Palgrave Studies in Cyberpsychology

Series Editor
Jens Binder
Nottingham Trent University
Nottingham, UK

Palgrave Studies in Cyberpsychology aims to foster and to chart the scope of research driven by a psychological understanding of the effects of the 'new technology' that is shaping our world after the digital revolution. The series takes an inclusive approach and considers all aspects of human behaviours and experiential states in relation to digital technologies, to the Internet, and to virtual environments. As such, Cyberpsychology reaches out to several neighbouring disciplines, from Human-Computer Interaction to Media and Communication Studies. A core question underpinning the series concerns the actual psychological novelty of new technology. To what extent do we need to expand conventional theories and models to account for cyberpsychological phenomena? At which points is the ubiquitous digitisation of our everyday lives shifting the focus of research questions and research needs? Where do we see implications for our psychological functioning that are likely to outlast shortlived fashions in technology use?

More information about this series at
http://www.palgrave.com/gp/series/14636

Michel Walrave • Joris Van Ouytsel
Koen Ponnet • Jeff R. Temple
Editors

Sexting

Motives and risk in online sexual self-presentation

Editors
Michel Walrave
Department of Communication
Studies, MIOS
University of Antwerp
Antwerp, Belgium

Joris Van Ouytsel
Department of Communication
Studies, MIOS
University of Antwerp
Antwerp, Belgium

Koen Ponnet
Department of Communication
Sciences, IMEC-MICT
Ghent University
Ghent, Belgium

Jeff R. Temple
Department of Ob/Gyn
UTMB Health
Galveston, TX, USA

Palgrave Studies in Cyberpsychology
ISBN 978-3-030-10126-8   ISBN 978-3-319-71882-8   (eBook)
https://doi.org/10.1007/978-3-319-71882-8

Cover illustration: © Stephen Bonk/Fotolia.co.uk

Printed on acid-free paper

This Palgrave Macmillan imprint is published by Springer Nature
The registered company is Springer International Publishing AG
The registered company address is: Gewerbestrasse 11, 6330 Cham, Switzerland

PREFACE

In the unfolding debate around the potential consequences of sexting, we aim to provide a nuanced account of the motives, contexts, and potential risks of this emerging phenomenon.

This book is the result of collaborations among experts from different disciplines including health sciences, communication studies, psychology, criminology, and law, and brings together complementary perspectives on sexting. The authors contribute to ongoing discussions around sexting by offering insights based on their own research and other international and interdisciplinary research. The authors are members of research teams that have built experience in the study of adolescents' uses of digital media from several scientific viewpoints. The legal and criminological aspects are investigated by authors from the Sydney Institute of Criminology (University of Sydney), University of New South Wales' (UNSW) Criminology and Criminal Justice team, and the School of Social Sciences, also in collaboration with the Human Rights Centre at Ghent University. The health-related issues are investigated by the Behavioral Health and Research (BHAR) team of the University of Texas Medical Branch (UTMB). The communicative and psychological facets of sexting are investigated by the research group MIOS at the University of Antwerp. Researchers from both BHAR and MIOS have worked together on projects relating to sexting and other digital risk behaviours such as cyber dating abuse with the support of travel and research grants awarded by the Research Foundation—Flanders and by the Fulbright Commission in Belgium, which allowed us to establish this collaboration. Collaborations were also arranged in the framework of the HealthNar (Health Narratives) network funded by the International Research Staff Exchange Scheme (IRSES) of Marie Curie Actions within the European Commission's Seventh Framework Programme. The research of all teams and their collaboration within current research projects and networks resulted in the present book.

The main purpose of this book is to move beyond the "moral panic" approach that often dominates the discourses on sexting. Our approach is grounded in situating sexting as being a part of adolescents' and adults' ways of expressing romantic or sexual interest. At the same time, we acknowledge the risks that intimate self-disclosures through digital media may induce. The first chapters of the book are therefore focused on the role sexting may play in romantic relationships, the opportunities and motives for sharing intimate digital images, and how it can be situated in the current media culture. Next to the positive and potential negative consequences which individuals may experience when sharing intimate pictures, this book also pays attention to the broader context in which sexting takes place. In the case of adolescents, we focus on the role parents may play in making their children aware of sexting-related consequences. Other chapters focus on how the media are covering sexting and how legislators try to regulate the negative consequences of sexting.

The introductory chapter discusses the origins of sexting, and more particularly the societal and scientific debate surrounding this behaviour. Sexting is first and foremost seen as a digital version of an old tendency to create and share sexual imagery. Michel Walrave and his co-authors argue that sexting can be seen as a normal behaviour, a novel form of the expressions of romantic interest and desire. However, sexting can be considered as problematic when it occurs under pressure or when the images are further distributed beyond the original sender's will. The risks of unwanted distribution are also linked with the characteristics of digital media. Therefore, this chapter explores the affordances of digital media that can facilitate intimate self-disclosures and that can lead to potential risks. Personal data shared through digital media are persistent, visible, spreadable, and searchable online. These characteristics are discussed within current debates on so-called ephemeral content apps. The authors also focus on how these characteristics influence the manipulation of digital images and, secondary sexting, the transmission of an entrusted sexting image to others. Next, the inhibitions to share intimate details or to transmit entrusted sexting messages may be lowered through individuals' online disinhibition. This may stimulate some individuals to be more open to engaging in intimate forms of communication. Others may experience less boundaries for criticizing or forwarding a sexting message, as they may not realize these online acts could have offline consequences. The authors further discuss how individuals deal with how privacy expectations are negotiated between individuals who engage in sexting. Consequently, this introductory chapter ends with the tension that may exist between the privacy of the depicted individual and the motives others may have when distributing this intimate personal information.

In the second chapter Lara Hallam and co-authors discuss sexting within the context of romantic relationships. Digital media, and more particularly social media apps, play an increasingly important role in individuals' dating behaviour. The authors begin their chapter by discussing different approaches to computer-mediated communication characterized by a reduction of physical cues. Online daters are therefore limited in the ways they can express themselves. However, this cues-filtered-out approach has been challenged by other theories that are part of the cues-filtered-in approach stating that computer-mediated communication may surpass face-to-face communication in some circumstances. In fact, the absence of nonverbal cues may stimulate people to search for other information to compensate. Moreover, the absence of nonverbal cues may be liberating and, therefore, online daters may be inclined to share more intimate information, such as sexting images. Online daters may also strategically create or alter their online self-presentation to maximize the chances of attaining their goal. Presenting oneself in an attractive way is important to attain potential daters. Nevertheless, as online dating environments may include impression management in an anonymous online environment, building trust and reducing uncertainty concerning a potential date is important. Therefore, online dating platforms have taken initiatives to reduce risks. Especially as online daters may share intimate information, including sexting pictures.

Why individuals, engaged in online dating, a romantic relationship, or otherwise, exchange intimate pictures, is the focus of the next chapter. Joris Van Ouytsel and co-authors explore the motives for sexting based on a review of quantitative as well as qualitative studies. The authors argue that sexting can be seen as a digital extension of the general human tendency to create sexually explicit images. The chapter outlines the different motives that lead adolescents and adults to engage in sexting in as well as outside the contexts of a romantic relationship. These contexts range from creating and sustaining intimacy to being a gateway to actual sexual behaviour. The authors further highlight the role of media socialization through the consumption of sexualized media and sexually explicit media, as an influencing factor in sexting behaviour. Research has also found that sexting can occur under pressure from peers or romantic partners, or, in more extreme cases, as a result of coercion. Although the literature tends to be focused on negative motives to engage in sexting, the authors also provide a state-of-the-art of research on the potential positive effects of sexting for interpersonal relationships.

Next to studying individuals' motives for engaging in sexting, much of the scientific research is also devoted to the risk behaviours that are associated with sexting, such as unsafe sex. Jeff Temple and Yu Lu review the evidence examining the associations between sexting and sexual (risk) behaviours, but also how it relates to psychological health. They describe that next to merely investigating the correlational associations, the focus on temporal relationships is important as well: Does sexting lead to sexual behaviour or do young people who have sex feel more comfortable to flirt through sexting? The same question holds for the potential link between sexting and risk behaviours, like substance use and sexual risk behaviours. Investigating these temporal relationships is important to guide prevention and education programmes, to empower adolescents to make informed decisions, and to cope with a partner's pressure. The authors conclude their chapter by stressing the need to integrate sexting as a topic in teaching young people healthy relationship skills, and to teach them the skills needed to take sexting-related risks into account when deciding to engage in sexting.

Next to formal education, parents also have an important role in informing and supporting youth in developing healthy relationship skills. The following chapter therefore focuses on how parents may engage in conversations about sexting. Ini Vanwesenbeeck and co-authors start by situating the role sexting can play during adolescence. While adolescents deepen relationships with friends and engage in romantic relationships, at the same time, they become more independent from their parents. It may therefore be challenging for parents to engage in conversations on sensitive topics such as sexting. On the one hand parents want to respect their child's autonomy, but on the other hand they want to prevent them from risks that may cause harm. In this chapter, the authors provide evidence that parents can play a role in educating their children concerning sexting-related risks. Surprisingly, scant research has investigated the relationships between parenting and children's sexting behaviour. Therefore the chapter first reviews theory and research on parenting styles in general, and parental internet mediation strategies in particular. The authors discuss several parenting styles that differ in terms of parental warmth and control and how they relate to children's development and behaviour. These insights into parents' roles are further linked with how this relates to adolescents' sexting behaviour. The role of mothers and fathers in childrearing and how it may possibly differ between their boys and girls is discussed. The focus is then shifted to strategies that parents may employ to mediate their child's digital media use, and the effectiveness of parental mediation strategies. Parents are also confronted with the fact that sexting behaviour and related risks are difficult to detect, due to their children's private use of mobile apps. Moreover, specific (restrictive) parental mediation strategies may result in reactance, countering parents' desired behaviours. Parents might also find it hard to discuss sex-related topics with their teenage children. The chapter ends with recommendations on how to address sexting. Open communication between parents and their children about sexting is imperative, so that teenagers feel comfortable opening up about their problems if they are confronted with the negative consequences of sexting.

One of the potential negative consequences of sexting is "slut-shaming". Individuals engaging in (online) sexual activities, such as the posting or sharing of sexual images may be criticized or harassed. In the next chapter, Kathleen Van Royen and colleagues investigate how social networking sites may induce this kind of risk, more particularly for female users. First, the authors contextualize sexting in the so-called sexual double standard, which rewards males for sexual activity while condemning girls who engage in the same behaviour. Slut-shaming is further discussed as an instrument of some girls to boost one's self-esteem, to position oneself within the peer group, or to express envy towards attractive girls. Among male adolescents, slut-shaming is linked with efforts to reinforce their masculinity or to regulate power relationships between male and female adolescents. Slut-shaming may even be raging on social media as some adolescents want to present themselves in accordance to male or female stereotypes. While this is often done with the aim of gaining popularity among the opposite sex, it may also lead to negative comments from peers. This chapter further presents research on the prevalence and correlates of slut-shaming, and the characteristics of teenage victims. Moreover, victims were also asked to report the event and the reasons they considered to have motivated the perpetrator. The authors conclude by addressing recommendations for parents, schools, and media. Popular media's role in the objectification of women and social media's responsibility in strengthening their online safety and reporting measures is highlighted.

Whereas the previous chapter addressed media's role in female objectivation, the next chapter analyses the attention media give to sexting in general and sexting-related incidents. As sexting is a highly debated topic, even soap operas have come to integrate the topic in their storylines. Alyce McGovern and Murray Lee analyse how the media, soap operas as well as press articles cover sexting motives and its potential consequences. They observe that teenage sexting is often covered by the media as being "problematic", and that the potential of sexting to cause embarrassment and legal consequences is often emphasized. These media discourses are analysed by exploring the most important sexting-related themes that emerged in analyses of media content on sexting in the UK and Australia. The authors discern several topics that dominate media reports on sexting, such as its prevalence, or the discourse which frames sexting as "epidemic" and feeds the moral panic surrounding it. Moreover, the authors have observed a gendered coverage of sexting, depicting different motives and consequences for girls and boys who engage in sexting. Young people are also portrayed in the media as lacking understanding of sexting consequences. References are made to young people's cognitive development, the importance of peer influence, and their impulsiveness, while parents and educators are encouraged to surveil their teenager and to discourage them to engage in sexting. Still, the authors also observe a tendency to nuanced discourses, for instance on the appropriateness of criminalizing sexting. These legal consequences, as well as the difference in legislative approaches, are further analysed in the final chapter.

Finally, Thomas Crofts and Eva Lievens contrast Europe's and Australia's legal approaches. While some governments have adopted legislation concerning child abuse and child pornography to protect minors, some tend to criminalize minors for their sexting behaviours. By contrast, others state that only some consequences, like the unauthorized distribution of sexting images, need to be legislated. The authors first analyse the international legislative framework, such as the UN Convention of the Rights of the Child and also the UN protocol recommending law reforms to criminalize children's sexual exploitation, including the exploitation of child abuse images. Next, the Commonwealth and state/territory legislation in Australia dealing with child pornography is discussed. The broad definitions included in this child pornography legislation have raised concerns for prosecutions of minors who engage in sexting. This legislative approach is contrasted with the European legislative framework. European conventions dealing with child pornography are reviewed. The authors highlight the fact that member states may exclude sexually explicit images that minors, who have reached the age of sexual consent, have produced and possess with consent and that are not further distributed. The same nuanced approach is found in the European directive on combating the sexual abuse and exploitation of children and child pornography. Again, the legislator tries to exclude consensual sexting. Next, the authors highlight other national legislative initiatives that have been taken, especially to address the non-consensual dissemination of sexual images. The authors further call for the need to create prevention and intervention initiatives to raise awareness about legal provisions, as well as to develop young people's—and adults'—resilience when pressured to engage in sexting. In many cases, sexting is a normal part of adolescents' exploration of their sexuality. As highlighted throughout this book, educational and other awareness-raising initiatives have to be implemented to assist young people in developing their sexual agency, being able to resist pressure, and being aware of potential consequences of sexting.

Through this unique collection of complementary research perspectives from well-established researchers from different regions of the world, this book aims to inspire the current debates that surround sexting. We hope that it will have a lasting impact on how sexting is discussed in educational initiatives and that it will inspire and inform the legislative initiatives taken in this context. Most importantly, we hope that this work might provide a stepping stone for future research, as we push forward in gaining a deeper understanding of sexting behaviour.

Michel Walrave
Joris Van Ouytsel
Koen Ponnet
Jeff R. Temple

Notes on Contributors

Thomas Crofts is Professor of Criminal Law and Director of the Sydney Institute of Criminology in the School of Law, The University of Sydney. His research in criminal law, criminology and criminal justice centres on criminalisation and criminal responsibility with a particular focus on the criminal responsibility of, and for, children, comparative criminal law and criminal law reform.

Charlotte De Backer is Associate Professor at the University of Antwerp, Department of Communication Studies. She teaches and conducts research in the domain of interpersonal relations. In her PhD (Ghent University) and postdoctoral research (UC Santa Barbara) she studied the various functions of interpersonal and celebrity gossip. One of the current topics of her research focuses on the sharing of reputation information by means of gossip on the perceived levels of trust in interpersonal relations.

Lara Hallam works as a teaching and research Assistant at the Department of Communication Studies of the University of Antwerp. As a doctoral student she is a member of the MIOS research group. Her research focusses on relationships that develop in online dating on the one hand, and on how online dating platforms can be enhanced to improve the initial interactions between potential romantic partners on the other hand.

Murray Lee is a Professor in Criminology at the University of Sydney Law School. He is the author of *Inventing Fear of Crime: Criminology and the Politics of Anxiety*, co-author of *Policing and Media: Public Relations,*

Simulations and Communications and *Sexting and Young People*, co-editor of *Fear of Crime: Critical Voices in an Age of Anxiety*, and editor of the scholarly journal *Current Issues in Criminal Justice*.

Eva Lievens is Assistant Professor of Law & Technology at the Law Faculty of Ghent University and a member of the Human Rights Centre. A recurrent focus in her research relates to human and children's rights in the ICT and media sector and the use of alternative regulatory instruments, such as self- and co-regulation.

Yu Lu is a postdoctoral Research Fellow at UTMB Health in Galveston, Texas. She received her doctorate in Communication Arts and Sciences from the Pennsylvania State University. Her major research interests are health decision-making and health disparities, particularly in the context of risk behaviours such as violence and substance abuse.

Alyce McGovern is a Senior Lecturer in Criminology in the School of Social Sciences, UNSW Sydney. She has researched widely in the area of crime and media, including police-media relations, police use of social media, and young people and sexting. She is the co-author of *Policing and Media: Public Relations, Simulations and Communications* and *Sexting and Young People*.

Karolien Poels is a Professor at the Department of Communication Studies of the University of Antwerp (Belgium). She studies individuals' uses and experiences of ICT and social media and how these insights can be applied for persuasive communication (advertising, protection and empowerment of consumers).

Koen Ponnet is an Assistant Professor at the Ghent University. He also teaches at the University of Antwerp. He is (co-)author of multiple articles on the determinants of online and offline health and risk behaviours of adolescents and adults. In his research, he also pays attention to the situation of vulnerable groups, like those who are at risk of poverty.

Jeff R. Temple is a Professor at UTMB Health in Galveston, Texas. He received his doctorate in counselling psychology from the University of North Texas and a postdoctoral research fellowship at Brown University. His major research interests include the aetiology, course, consequences, prevention, and treatment of intimate partner and teen dating violence.

Heidi Vandebosch is Professor at the Department of Communication Studies at the University of Antwerp (Belgium). Her research mainly focuses on cyberbullying (prevalence, profiles of bullies and victims, impact, evidence-based interventions, the role of schools, the police and news media).

Joris Van Ouytsel is a postdoctoral Researcher at the Department of Communication Studies at the University of Antwerp. He focuses his research on the influence of digital media on relationship experiences and sexuality among adolescents. More specifically, he investigates the role of sexting and cyber dating abuse, the use of digital media within romantic relationship to control or harass a romantic partner.

Kathleen Van Royen is a postdoctoral Researcher at the Department of Communication Studies at the University of Antwerp (Belgium). She conducts research on social networking sites and cyber harassment, in particular sexual harassment and adolescents.

Ini Vanwesenbeeck graduated in 2010 as a Master in Communication Sciences at the University of Antwerp. After graduation, Ini participated in several short projects on eSafety and cyberbullying at the University of Antwerp. In October 2011, Ini obtained a PhD Fellowship from the Research Foundation – Flanders (FWO). Her doctoral thesis, supervised by Prof. dr. Michel Walrave and Prof. dr. Koen Ponnet, focussed on embedded online advertising targeted at children, in which she investigated amongst other parental media mediation and advertising. Currently, Ini works at Ghent University as project coordinator for AdLit, a research project funded by VLAIO.

Michel Walrave is a Professor at the Department of Communication Studies, University of Antwerp. He is responsible for the research group MIOS. His research is centered around online self-disclosure and privacy. He investigates adolescents' and adults' online disclosure of personal information to other individuals, including intimate self-disclosures such as sexting. Next, he investigates individuals' entrusting of personal information to companies, and related opportunities and risks.

CONTENTS

CHAPTER 1

Sharing and Caring? The Role of Social Media and Privacy in Sexting Behaviour

Michel Walrave, Joris Van Ouytsel, Koen Ponnet,
and Jeff R. Temple

Abstract In this introductory chapter, we explore the debate surrounding intimate self-disclosures through social media. Discussions concerning sexting and sexting related incidents are associated with social media affordances. In particular, we investigate how digital media content's persistence, visibility, spreadability and searchability are linked to challenges that individuals may face when sexting. Next, we examine how sexting behaviours can be understood through the lens of online

M. Walrave (✉) • J. Van Ouytsel
Department of Communication Studies, MIOS, University of Antwerp,
Antwerp, Belgium

K. Ponnet
Department of Communication Studies, MIOS, University of Antwerp,
Antwerp, Belgium

Department of Communication Sciences, IMEC-MICT, Ghent University,
Ghent, Belgium

J. R. Temple
Department of Obstetrics Gynecology, Behavioral Health and Research, UTMB,
Galveston, TX, USA

© The Author(s) 2018
M. Walrave et al. (eds.), *Sexting*, Palgrave Studies in Cyberpsychology,
https://doi.org/10.1007/978-3-319-71882-8_1

disinhibition, as this may lower thresholds for intimate forms of communication. Finally, once a sexting message is sent, it involves individuals who share (or do not share) the same objectives and values concerning the intimate information they co-own. The Communication Privacy Management theory provides a framework to understand sexting as a shared responsibility.

Keywords Sexting • Online disinhibition • Communication privacy management theory • Social media affordances

INTRODUCTION

Individuals have long used media in creative ways to share intimate feelings. From love letters, intimate diaries, Polaroid pictures, to a series of smartphone apps, they all offer individuals opportunities to express romantic interest and sustain intimacy. Sexting, the sending of self-made sexually explicit messages through digital media, is a modern incarnation of a long development of uses of media for romantic and sexual expression. Through smartphone and social media apps, individuals can easily create and share intimate messages. At the advent of cellular technology, intimate mobile messaging was limited to text and emoticons. In recent years, photos, videos and emoji have offered a broader range of possibilities to express oneself visually. Emoji are sometimes even manipulated to communicate their own sexting language, with flowers and vegetables as visual metaphors (Evans, 2017). Because of these changes in technological capabilities, the meaning of the term 'sexting' has also rapidly evolved. While originally a combination of 'sex' and 'texting', the development of smartphones and other devices have expanded sexting to include sexual imagery.

Although sexting is merely a digital extension of the age-old human tendency to create sexually explicit images, visual forms of sexting are also a source of concern, as digital images can easily be disseminated to a wider audience. The further distribution of intimate photographs has led to tragic cases. For example, when a sexting image spreads to a broader audience, it can lead to bullying and reputational damage for the person who has created the sexting message. Often victims of these incidents are blamed for creating these types of photographs in the first place, as doing so made them vulnerable for the abuse. The early literature on sexting treats the creation of sexually explicit images as a deviant behaviour (see for an overview e.g., Döring, 2014; Kosenko, Luurs, & Binder, 2017). However, scholars and prevention workers have argued that the mere creation of sexting photographs can be considered normal. Moreover, in recent years, research on sexting behaviour has also observed its positive role in relationship satisfaction (Burkett, 2015; Drouin, Coupe, & Temple, 2017). Nowadays, sexting is only considered to be problematic, when it occurs under pressure, is the result of coercion, or if the content is distributed without authorization (Choi, Van Ouytsel, & Temple, 2016; Temple, 2015).

The tendency to blame the individuals who sext, rather than blaming individuals who breach the trust or engage in abusive behaviours, can be partly situated in some media, policy and even academic discourses which tend to neglect individuals', and more particularly young people's, agency to make deliberate and sensible choices regarding their sexuality and sexual intimacy. Young people, and particularly girls, are seen as a passive audience or even victims of sexualization trends in popular media content. This leads to a lot of efforts to convince potential sexters to refrain, as they are the potential authors of sexualized content, which could be used against them (Spooner & Vaughn, 2016).

In this context, sexting is often associated with the sexualization of media culture, the proliferation of sexualized images and discussions on sexual practices (Gill, 2012). However, pointing at, or even blaming, media's sexual content can contextualize individuals' sharing of intimate messages, but might also distract from discussing core issues within sexual and broader relational ethics namely mutual consent, pleasure and respect (Carmody, 2005). Sexting incidents are often related with, on the one hand, pressure or even abuse within intimate relationships or, on the other hand, privacy breaches (Hasinoff, 2014). Framing sexting as inherently harmful stifles young people's potential for sexual exploration, but reframing sexting as normal behaviour while acknowledging that it bears some level of risk offers young people a level of agency to decide for themselves (Lim, 2013). To be able to make informed decisions, not only the relational context wherein sexting occurs is important, but also individuals' knowledge about the specific characteristics of digital media they use for intimate communication.

Social Media Affordances

In order to explore the opportunities for intimate self-disclosure that social media provide, as well as the potential risks associated with it, we build upon the affordances framework proposed by boyd (2011, 2014). As sexting content is transmitted one-to-one through, for instance, mobile media apps, they are shared within a networked public which differs from traditional publics in offline spaces. Four affordances shape the context of social media and how self-disclosures, especially intimate ones, may be facilitated or challenged. Those affordances of digital media are persistence, visibility, spreadability and searchability.

Digital data in general, and digitally transmitted images in particular, may become persistent. What has been sent in a snap, may be stored and transmitted to others, now or later. Even some applications that are considered safe for sexting, in which images disappear after a set amount of time, can be bypassed through technical tricks or third-party apps. For instance, security breaches in third-party providers' systems led to the online publication of thousands of images shared through the popular instant messaging application Snapchat, from which a significant proportion were sexually explicit pictures (Piwek & Joinson, 2016). Not only can a sexting message be stored and potentially forwarded to others, but also it may resurface later, for instance on websites or closed groups in social network sites where those pictures are 'exposed'. The persistence of social media content may lead to a context collapse, for instance, when personal information that was shared with only one, or several other contacts, for specific purposes is taken out of context and reaches other individuals (Marwick & boyd, 2014). Moreover, if the relationship sours, the messages that were once protected may be used against its creator (Mitchell, Finkelhor, Jones, & Wolak, 2012).

In this context, the exposure of what once was an intimate message secretly shared between partners may become visible for an unintended audience. Whereas in the offline world audiences may be more visible and sizeable, in online networks, "interactions are often public by default, private through effort" (boyd, 2014, p. 14). However, privacy settings and other security measures provide only an illusory sense of control over one's personal information. First, privacy settings regulate only some aspects of personal information visibility with respect to other social media users. Second, although users may limit a message's audience, it is not guaranteed that one of those trusted parties will not share this content with individuals that were not intended in the first place. However, technological responses such as photo DNA are being developed. By computing hash values, a specific photo receives a unique hash, in other words, a digital fingerprint which is even resistant to some alterations of the image (like resizing or altering the colour). If the original image is further distributed, it can be tracked and blocked with the collaboration of the site's provider. While this technology is currently used for tracking and taking down child abuse images (Microsoft, 2017), it could potentially have other applications. For instance, an intimate image that was publicly spread and that police forces have in their database could, in the future, be tracked and taken down.

In sexting-related incidents, the spreadability of what originally was meant as an intimate exchange, adds to the victim's distress as it is not clear who has seen the picture, whether it will be further distributed and if it will pop up at a later stage in life. As digital content may be permanent and easy to forward, there is a possibility for repeated victimization when new individuals discover the disclosed message (Peskin et al., 2017).

Technologies offer widespread possibilities to search for information. Intimate messages linked to an identifiable person or online news reports of a sexting incident can live in perpetuity for current and future audiences to watch. The ease with which digitalized data can be stored and distributed is also something to keep in mind when discussing sexting or online disclosures of personal information in general.

Moreover, in an era of bits, an original picture is sometimes undistinguishable from its copy (boyd, 2011). Digital content that is transmitted can be altered. Pictures can be manipulated in ways only detectable by an expert eye. As one study reveals, secondary sexting, i.e. the transmission of an entrusted sexting picture to others, may not only revolve around an original sexting picture that was sent. In this study adolescents reported on an incident where a sexting picture was spread across several schools. After a breakup, the ex-boyfriend distributed pictures of his ex-girlfriend. He mixed pictures of the victim lightly clothed, with pornographic pictures that he found online in order to create the impression that his ex-girlfriend also sent these sexually explicit pictures. In sum, a sexting incident can also revolve around the fabrication of a sexting picture or creating the impression that someone has engaged in sexting, not only the further distribution of an original one (Van Ouytsel, Van Gool, Walrave, Ponnet, & Peeters, 2016).

Although the aforementioned affordances of digital media do not predict how (social) media users will communicate, they do shape the context of their communication. Moreover, next to characteristics of digital data, the focus of discussions about sexting also includes the ways in which individuals possibly behave differently online than offline.

FEELING DISINHIBITED

Do we behave differently online? This is the central question that led researchers to investigate the online disinhibition effect. The main focus in Suler's concept is the observation that some people loosen up when online, and are tempted to do or say things they would refrain from doing or saying when face-to-face with another individual (Suler, 2004).

This disinhibition can be beneficial, as individuals may open up and disclose thoughts and feelings or offer help and advice online, which would be more difficult for them to do offline. This is called "benign disinhibition" (Suler, 2004, p. 321). For instance, it may be easier for individuals who experience difficulties expressing their romantic interest to send a digital message instead of confronting the direct reactions of the person they long for. Not being directly confronted with the judging look of others, may lower thresholds to self-disclose one's innermost feelings (Kowalski & Limber, 2007). In this context, researchers found that the more adolescents perceived that instant messaging offered them more control over the interaction, and the more they perceived the reduced non-verbal cues during instant messaging to be relevant, the more they were disinhibited to talk freely online and, subsequently, engaged more in online self-disclosure about feelings, sex and other intimate topics (Schouten, Valkenburg, & Peter, 2007).

However, since most digital media applications strip away non-verbal cues, such as intonation, facial expressions, or body language, messages shared through these media may also be misinterpreted and lead to misunderstandings (Heirman & Walrave, 2008). For instance, a lack of non-verbal cues has been linked to harassment such as cyberbullying (Kowalski, Limber, & Agatston, 2012). In other words, also negative expressions of this disinhibition effect are witnessed (referred to as "toxic disinhibition" (Suler, 2004, p. 321)). Cyberbullying, cyber dating abuse, trolling, and other forms of aggressive behaviour are unfortunately a part of individuals' experiences online, as either the victim or a bystander of these aggressions. As digital communication creates a distance between the persons involved, emotional feedback is missing or delayed. The senders of the messages may be less inclined to modulate their tone. Therefore, message senders may not realize the impact they have. Conversely, being eye-to-eye may cause potential perpetrators to pause when they see their aggressions having an impact on the victims and the witnesses. A victim's direct emotional responses (such as frowning or tears) might augment the inhibitions of perpetrators to engage in abusive behaviours as they are able to assess the impact of their words and actions.

Both benign and toxic disinhibition may be interpreted as an 'electronic wall' that prevents senders from immediately detecting the receiver's (emotional) reactions. Perpetrators may feel 'dissociated', not realizing that their acts in a virtual space may have an impact in real life. Moreover, perpetrators may not be aware of their 'audience' when, for instance, they engage in public forms of cyberbullying on social network sites (Bernstein, Bakshy, Burke, & Karrer, 2013). This would allow people to communicate more freely with each other without fear of direct consequences (Kowalski et al., 2012).

It's important to highlight that both directions of disinhibition are possible, not only negative ones. Individuals needing advice for personal problems may have a lower threshold in seeking online help or discussing issues with health professionals in online (anonymous) forums or chatrooms. For instance, when adolescents develop their identities and build their social networks, digital media may play an important role. Youth developing their identity may feel disinhibited in sharing their feelings, doubts and aspirations online, but may also seek and give advice or comfort. Especially social network sites may be used to present oneself, receive or offer feedback and expand one's social circle. Therefore, social network sites play a role in the developmental goals of adolescents, namely, in identity construction, achieving more autonomy (from their parents) and the development and deepening of friendships and romantic relationships (Jackson & Goossens, 2006; Steinberg & Morris, 2001). Young people have also been found to engage in online self-disclosure more than adults (Christofides, Muise, & Desmarais, 2012; Walrave, Vanwesenbeeck, & Heirman, 2012). Adolescents are triggered more by the short-term rewards and they are less inclined to think of potential consequences of their online disclosures (Albert & Steinberg, 2011). Moreover, the characteristics of some digital media can trigger disinhibition. In some social network sites that group offline social networks with new online acquaintances, individuals communicate using their personal identity, while other social network apps give users the possibility to create anonymous profiles. This can set the stage for "dissociative anonymity" where digital media users dissociate the behaviours of their online persona from their in-person identity. By doing so, they can distance themselves from real-life rules and social conventions. They may feel less vulnerable to self-disclose or to react to other users' self-disclosures (Suler, 2004, p. 322). While Suler referred to games in this context, now, more than a decade later, dating and instant communication apps may offer a similar context where users feel safe behind their online personas.

Next to the aspect of invisibility, digital communication's asynchronicity might be another disinhibiting factor in sexting behaviour, as it provides individuals with time to reflect and reply. When sending an intimate message, not having to cope with the receiver's immediate reaction may be relieving (for a while). When engaging in secondary sexting, namely forwarding an entrusted intimate message, perpetrators can choose to disconnect and avoid confrontation with these actions' potential consequences.

In the digital world, other forms of social status apply. The digital world is less focused on traditional status and authority, but more so on how one handles the written word, knows how to influence or impact other individuals online and can use digital media in an impactful way. Online power differences may also be based on differences in 'technopower' (Jordan, 1999). For instance, how one can copy a Snapchat message without the sender noticing or how one can create a fake profile or online group for posting and sharing revenge porn. At the same time, digital competencies can be used to trace the perpetrators or to create supportive online spaces to assist a victim whose intimate messages have been abused.

Another characteristic of digital communication that may fuel online disinhibition is some individuals' ability to imagine the person one is communicating with online. People chatting online may construct characteristics and reactions of the other person by using what they know about that person (offline), pictures of that person, and/or based on their own imagination. The other person becomes part of one's mental world. Text messages and pictures forge this introjected character. What is communicated by that person can be further developed in an individual's mind through his/her own desires, wishes and previous experiences. "Online text communication can evolve into an introjected psychological tapestry in which a person's mind weaves these fantasy role plays, usually unconsciously and with considerable disinhibition" (Suler, 2004, p. 323). In the context of sexting, individuals may fantasize about the partner, draw conclusions from interpretations of received text messages, or construct elaborate scripts about how it might feel to be close with that person. Free of boundaries but the limits of one's own imagination, conversations and actions can be fantasized.

Furthermore, characteristics of specific digital applications may facilitate or discourage disinhibition. The facilitation of disinhibition may be enhanced by the promise that a message will be 'destroyed' after a set time limit. With respect to discouraging disinhibition, users may receive more time to reflect on a message or be warned about the content of the message and the potential consequences of sending messages in certain circumstances or during late or early hours. An example of the former revolves around reflective interfaces, which automatically detect words or images and invite a user to reflect on his or her behaviour. This is obtained by presenting a cue, when specific (textual or visual) information is automatically detected (Dinakar, Jones, Havasi, Lieberman, & Picard, 2012). The user can still decide to continue, so their freedom of expression is respected, but reflection is stimulated. In other words, before posting an intimate (textual or visual) message, this reflection phase could be integrated. Additionally, before an aggressive reaction is posted, a reflective cue could remind the social media user of the potential audience and the action's possible consequences (e.g., when the acceptable use policy is infringed). However, some perpetrators may be stimulated by the perspective of the audience they would reach (Van Royen, Poels, Vandebosch, & Adam, 2017).

Applications that let users set a time frame in which they cannot text a specific list of numbers are examples of the latter. This 'drunk mode' prevents smartphone users from sending messages for a couple of hours by temporarily 'blacklisting' business partners or family members. This prohibits the user from sending blurry-eyed selfies, naked images, or other potentially harmful messages (Resnick, 2016). While this technique does offer a rapid on-the-spot solution, it does not promote a reflective process regarding this behaviour.

Although there are applications developed to assist smartphone users in deciding to send (or not to send) a text message or picture, these apps are less adapted in the sharing of intimate messages within a romantic relationship. The swapping of sexting messages within a romantic, or other relational context, still remains a shared responsibility.

Sexting, a Shared Responsibility

When referring to sexting as a form of intimate self-disclosure, the act of entrusting this form of personal information to someone creates a shared responsibility. The affordances of social media that facilitate the transmission of entrusted messages highlight the need to find common ground between partners in the boundaries of this intimate digital communication. How individuals negotiate these boundaries, is enlightened by the Communication Privacy Management Theory (CPM) developed by Petronio (2002).

One of CPM's tenets is that individuals believe they own information related to them and are therefore convinced they are entitled to control this information (Petronio, 2013). When an individual grants access to his/her personal information, others become (authorized) co-owners, forming a mutual privacy boundary surrounding this shared personal information. However, when personal information is shared, individuals (i.e., the original owners) believe they keep the rights to their personal information and, therefore, they want to further control the access to it. Hence, senders and receivers may have to negotiate or co-construct (privacy) rules concerning the information they mutually hold (Petronio, 2016). As a result, individuals develop a set of rules based on principles or values that are important to them. Some of the rules are stable and influenced by core criteria based on one's culture, gender or other characteristics (Petronio, 2013, 2016). Within a romantic relationship, for instance, both partners bring their own sets of rules based on their individual privacy orientations and learned or negotiated in their own families. As these rules may differ, romantic partners negotiate and merge their rules, as they become co-owners of personal information they share as a couple (Petronio, 2013). Sharing personal information with one's partner therefore includes (implicitly or explicitly) some obligations for the recipient concerning (potential) third-party dissemination. Consequently, when entrusting personal information, a disclosure warning may be added as a privacy rule regulating the disclosure, warning the entrusted individual if and, in that case, who may be legitimately included in the privacy boundary and who is excluded from it (Petronio, 2010). Next to the couple's external privacy boundary, internal privacy boundaries exist. Depending on the need to protect some personal information, a partner may keep some information to him/herself or establish a privacy boundary with a close friend who is not his/her partner.

In sum, CPM highlights the notion that privacy is not seclusion, but the choice of keeping information for oneself or entrusting it with selected others. This principle echoes Altman's words, "Privacy is the selective control of access to the self" (Altman, 1975, p. 24). CPM grasps this dialectic tension between individuals' access and privacy needs, which drives their privacy management choices (Child & Petronio, 2011). Moreover, privacy management concords with Alan Westin's classic definition of privacy as "the claim of individuals, groups or institutions to determine for themselves when, how, and to what extend information about them is communicated to others" (Westin, 1970, p. 7). Privacy is therefore not only the claim of an individual but also the claim of couples or other types of groups concerning the personal information they co-own within their shared privacy boundary.

Still, privacy boundaries evolve. Whenever an individual or a group of individuals entrust personal information with others, they reshape the privacy boundary (Griffin, Ledbetter, & Sparks, 2014). Through the disclosure of personal information, individuals become linked with each other in privacy boundaries (Petronio, 2004). Once personal information has been shared, the involved parties negotiate privacy rules for the possible sharing of this information with others. Within a couple, for instance, partners reveal personal information to each other in order to meet personal or relational needs. At the same time, they can decide to conceal information from their partner to keep it within a personal privacy boundary (Child & Petronio, 2011). A couple, or other group of individuals who collectively hold personal information, negotiate the privacy rules for (potential) third-party dissemination. Setting these co-ownership boundaries creates a backstage—a safe zone—to share personal matters within a romantic relationship. Next to discussing ideas, common projects or even fantasies may also be entrusted. Romantic partners negotiate the boundary rules and define whether personal information can be shared and with whom. In general, once someone has been granted access to personal information, privacy rules are coordinated and negotiated with the authorized co-owners to be able to continue to control third-party access to one's personal information. Correspondingly, co-owners hold and operate collective privacy boundaries. How much others may know, and how, if at all, they may further disseminate the information is regulated between them (Petronio, 2013).

Just like in a family, a team, or a group of friends, romantic partners become jointly responsible for regulating the permeability of their common privacy boundary, based on the agreed-upon rules for treating entrusted personal information (Petronio, Jones, & Morr, 2003). Romantic partners balance their need for individual autonomy with their relational intimacy by controlling the flow of information to each other (Petronio, 1991). Both partners need to agree on their privacy boundary permeability. This refers to how protected or porous the couple's privacy boundary is. For instance, how romantic partners come to an agreement on keeping the sexting messages to themselves. Still, if a case arises where one partner feels pressure to sext, he/she might confide in a friend in order to seek advice. How the confidant will treat this sensitive information once he/she is brought into the privacy boundary depends on personal characteristics, the history of the friendship and, possibly, whether both friends discuss the confidentiality of the entrusted information. If it is not clearly discussed what can or cannot be revealed and to who, privacy boundaries become blurred and permeable. Moreover, the confidant can feel torn between, on the one hand, keeping this secret or on the other hand, seeking extra advice by taking someone else in his/her confidence, to assist the friend who is pressured to sext.

Generally, how privacy boundary management between individuals is ruled can be facilitated by several factors. Petronio (2002) discerns five factors that come into play: culture, gender, motivation, context and risk/benefit calculations. The first factor pertains to cultural expectations concerning privacy in general, and respecting entrusted intimate messages in particular. Cultures may differ in individualism, uncertainty avoidance (Hofstede, 2001, 2011) and other characteristics which may play a role in how individuals deal with personal information. Gender, age, and personality type may also factor into an individual's decision to provide or withhold intimate messages. Furthermore, personal motivations may influence how individuals deal with their privacy boundaries. A person who is attracted to another individual may loosen his/her privacy boundary and engage in intimate disclosures (Griffin et al., 2014). Context is also an important factor. For instance, a romantic break-up and its impact may disrupt the rules or agreements made concerning the secrecy of shared intimate messages. One of the partners may struggle when coping with this romantic break-up and make these messages public for revenge (Van Ouytsel et al., 2016). This forms an intentional breach of the privacy boundary to hurt the intimate information's original owner.

In specific situations, individuals engage in a risk-benefit trade off by adding up the benefits and subtracting the potential risks in sharing or concealing personal information. For instance, will an individual hold the same respect for his/her (ex-) partner's privacy when peers pressure him/her to share the sext? How will possible sanctions for disclosing an (ex-) partner's personal information or other potential drawbacks be taken into account? How does sharing sexts among peers act as a kind of 'popularity currency' (Lippman & Campbell, 2014; Ringrose, Harvey, Gill, & Livingstone, 2013), and how would that play a role in this equation? Besides the possible roles third parties may play in divulging personal information, differences may exist between partners' expectations concerning their couple's privacy boundary. Moreover, when a couple parts ways, this could create what Petronio (2002) calls, privacy turbulence.

Privacy turbulence occurs when, intentionally or not, violations are made in the way co-owners regulate the flow of personal information with third parties (Petronio, 1991, 2002). Such privacy violations among partners or friends can impact the core of a relationship (Steuber & McLaren, 2015). Specific circumstances or actions by co-owners of the personal information may challenge the agreed upon privacy boundary. Moreover, an individual who originally owned the information may expect that co-owners, who are now part of the collective privacy boundary, will know and follow the privacy rules that were set (Child & Petronio, 2011). Co-owners who explicitly coordinate how shared personal information should be handled may reduce the chance of privacy turbulence (Petronio, 2016). However, are privacy expectations and rules made clear by the original owner of the personal information? Are these privacy rules shared with and agreed upon by the other co-owners? Do these rules compete with the motives co-owners might have when distributing this sensitive information?

If a sext originally shared between romantic partners, is transmitted to others, they become co-owners of that information and become co-responsible for managing this sensitive information. These new confidants are drawn into a collective privacy boundary, willingly or not (Griffin et al., 2014). The new recipients can decide to further distribute the sext message or to synchronize their privacy boundary coordination by deciding, for instance, to stop the further transmission of the message. Their co-ownership and corresponding co-responsibility is an important facet in stopping the dissemination of a sext message. This corresponds with the call for sexual, or broader relational ethics which places the responsibility for further dissemination of a sext not on its original sender but on those who breach the privacy boundaries and engage in secondary sexting. The impact of secondary sexting depends on how others react, transmit the message or stop the spreading of it, acting in solidarity with the original sender whose privacy was breached. Privacy turbulence can be seen as a relational transgression (Petronio, 2002; Steuber & McLaren, 2015). Such privacy violations are impactful and disruptive. However, next to the immediate negative impact that they may cause, privacy violations hold potentially positive outcomes (Petronio, 2010). Such critical moments can become occasions to reaffirm privacy rules or take other initiatives to recalibrate or re-coordinate the privacy rules and, possibly, prevent other privacy breakdowns (Child & Petronio, 2011).

Therefore, in the unfolding debate on sexting motives, it is important to examine the contexts and consequences of sexting, focussing not only on the creators of sexts but also on those who apply pressure to sext and on those who breach privacy boundaries. These target groups need to be kept in mind when designing prevention and intervention strategies, next to enhancing support for victims of non-consensual sexting as well as victims of secondary sexting.

References

Albert, D., & Steinberg, L. (2011). Judgment and decision making in adolescence: Adolescent JDM. *Journal of Research on Adolescence, 21*(1), 211–224. https://doi.org/10.1111/j.1532-7795.2010.00724.x.

Altman, I. (1975). *The environment and social behavior: Privacy, personal space, territory, crowding.* Monterey, CA: Brooks/Cole Publishing.

Bernstein, M. S., Bakshy, E., Burke, M., & Karrer, B. (2013). *Quantifying the invisible audience in social networks,* 21. ACM Press. doi:https://doi.org/10.1145/2470654.2470658.

boyd, d. (2011). Social network sites as networked publics: Affordances, dynamics, and implications. In *Networked self: Identity, community, and culture on social network sites* (pp. 39–58). New York: Routledge/Papacharissi, Z.

boyd, d. (2014). *It's complicated. The social lives of networked teens.* New Haven, London: Yale University Press.

Burkett, M. (2015). Sex(t) talk: A qualitative analysis of young adults' negotiations of the pleasures and perils of sexting. *Sexuality & Culture, 19*(4), 835–863. https://doi.org/10.1007/s12119-015-9295-0.

Carmody, M. (2005). Ethical Erotics: Reconceptualizing anti-rape education. *Sexualities, 8*(4), 465–480. https://doi.org/10.1177/1363460705056621.

Child, J. T., & Petronio, S. (2011). Unpacking the paradoxes of privacy in CMC relationships: The challenges of blogging and relational communication on the internet. In K. B. Wright & L. M. Webb (Eds.), *Computer-mediated communication in personal relationships* (pp. 21–40). New York: Peter Lang.

Choi, H., Van Ouytsel, J., & Temple, J. R. (2016). Association between sexting and sexual coercion among female adolescents. *Journal of Adolescence, 53,* 164–168. https://doi.org/10.1016/j.adolescence.2016.10.005.

Christofides, E., Muise, A., & Desmarais, S. (2012). Hey mom, What's on your Facebook? Comparing Facebook disclosure and privacy in adolescents and adults. *Social Psychological and Personality Science, 3*(1), 48–54. https://doi.org/10.1177/1948550611408619.

Dinakar, K., Jones, B., Havasi, C., Lieberman, H., & Picard, R. (2012). Common sense reasoning for detection, prevention, and mitigation of cyberbullying. *ACM Transactions on Interactive Intelligent Systems, 2*(3), 1–30. https://doi.org/10.1145/2362394.2362400.

Döring, N. (2014). Consensual sexting among adolescents: Risk prevention through abstinence education or safer sexting? *Cyberpsychology: Journal of Psychosocial Research on Cyberspace, 8*(1). https://doi.org/10.5817/CP2014-1-9.

Drouin, M., Coupe, M., & Temple, J. R. (2017). Is sexting good for your relationship? It depends .... *Computers in Human Behavior, 75,* 749–756. https://doi.org/10.1016/j.chb.2017.06.018.

Evans, V. (2017). *Emoji code. How smiley face, love hearts and thumbs up are changing the way we communicate.* London: Michael O'Mara Books.

Gill, R. (2012). The sexualisation of culture?: Sexualisation of culture? *Social and Personality Psychology Compass, 6*(7), 483–498. https://doi.org/10.1111/j.1751-9004.2012.00433.x.

Griffin, E., Ledbetter, A., & Sparks, G. (2014). Communication privacy management theory. In *A first look at communication theory* (pp. 151–163). New York: McGraw-Hill.

Hasinoff, A. A. (2014). Blaming sexualization for sexting. *Girlhood Studies, 7*(1). https://doi.org/10.3167/ghs.2014.070108.

Heirman, W., & Walrave, M. (2008). Assessing concerns and issues about the mediation of technology in cyberbullying. *Cyberpsychology: Journal of Psychosocial Research on Cyberspace, 2*(2), 1–12. https://cyberpsychology.eu/article/view/4214/3256.

Hofstede, G. (2001). *Culture's consequences. Comparing values, behaviors, institutions and organizations across nations.* Thousand Oaks, CA: Sage.

Hofstede, G. (2011). Dimensionalizing cultures: The Hofstede model in context. *Online Readings in Psychology and Culture, 2*(1). https://doi.org/10.9707/2307-0919.1014.

Jackson, S., & Goossens, L. (2006). *Handbook of adolescent development.* New York: Psychology Press.

Jordan, T. (1999). *Cyberpower. The culture and politics of cyberspace and the internet.* London: Routledge.

Kosenko, K., Luurs, G., & Binder, A. R. (2017). Sexting and sexual behavior, 2011–2015: A critical review and meta-analysis of a growing literature: Sexting and sexual behavior. *Journal of Computer-Mediated Communication, 22*(3), 141–160. https://doi.org/10.1111/jcc4.12187.

Kowalski, R. M., & Limber, S. P. (2007). Electronic bullying among middle school students. *Journal of Adolescent Health, 41*(6), S22–S30. https://doi.org/10.1016/j.jadohealth.2007.08.017.

Kowalski, R. M., Limber, S. P., & Agatston, P. W. (2012). *Cyber bullying: Bullying in the digital age.* Malden, MA: Wiley-Blackwell.

Lim, S. S. (2013). On mobile communication and youth "deviance": Beyond moral, media and mobile panics. *Mobile Media & Communication, 1*(1), 96–101. https://doi.org/10.1177/2050157912459503.

Lippman, J. R., & Campbell, S. W. (2014). Damned if you do, damned if you don't…If you're a girl: Relational and normative contexts of adolescent sexting in the United States. *Journal of Children and Media, 8*(4), 371–386. https://doi.org/10.1080/17482798.2014.923009.

Marwick, A. E., & boyd, d. (2014). Networked privacy: How teenagers negotiate context in social media. *New Media & Society, 16*(7), 1051–1067. https://doi.org/10.1177/1461444814543995.

Microsoft. (2017). PhototDNA cloud service. Retrieved from https://www.microsoft.com/en-us/photodna

Mitchell, K. J., Finkelhor, D., Jones, L. M., & Wolak, J. (2012). Prevalence and characteristics of youth sexting: A national study. *Pediatrics, 129*(1), 13–20. https://doi.org/10.1542/peds.2011-1730.

Peskin, M. F., Markham, C. M., Shegog, R., Temple, J. R., Baumler, E. R., Addy, R. C., et al. (2017). Prevalence and correlates of the perpetration of cyber dating abuse among early adolescents. *Journal of Youth and Adolescence, 46*(2), 358–375. https://doi.org/10.1007/s10964-016-0568-1.

Petronio, S. (1991). Communication boundary management: A theoretical model of managing disclosure of private information between marital couples. *Communication Theory, 1*(4), 311–335.

Petronio, S. (2002). *Boundaries of privacy: Dialectics of disclosure.* New York: State University of New York Press.

Petronio, S. (2004). Road to developing communication privacy management theory: Narrative in progress, please stand by. *Journal of Family Communication, 4*(3–4), 193–207. https://doi.org/10.1080/15267431.2004.9670131.

Petronio, S. (2010). Communication privacy management theory: What do we know about family privacy regulation? *Journal of Family Theory & Review, 2*(3), 175–196. https://doi.org/10.1111/j.1756-2589.2010.00052.x.

Petronio, S. (2013). Brief status report on communication privacy management theory. *Journal of Family Communication, 13*(1), 6–14. https://doi.org/10.1080/15267431.2013.743426.

Petronio, S. (2016). Communication privacy management. In K. B. Jensen, E. W. Rothenbuhler, J. D. Pooley, & R. T. Craig (Eds.), *The international encyclopedia of communication theory and philosophy* (pp. 1–9). Hoboken, NJ: Wiley. Retrieved from http://doi.wiley.com/10.1002/9781118766804.wbiect138.

Petronio, S., Jones, S., & Morr, M. C. (2003). Family privacy dilemmas: Managing communication boundaries within family groups. In L. Frey (Ed.), *Group communication in context: Studies of bona fide groups* (pp. 23–56). Mahwah, NJ: Lawrence Erlbaum Associates.

Piwek, L., & Joinson, A. (2016). "What do they snapchat about?" patterns of use in time-limited instant messaging service. *Computers in Human Behavior, 54*, 358–367. https://doi.org/10.1016/j.chb.2015.08.026.

Resnick, N. (2016, July 28). 3 Growth hacks that catapulted a "Drunk-Dialing" app to sober success. Retrieved from https://www.entrepreneur.com/article/279625

Ringrose, J., Harvey, L., Gill, R., & Livingstone, S. (2013). Teen girls, sexual double standards and "sexting": Gendered value in digital image exchange. *Feminist Theory, 14*(3), 305–323. https://doi.org/10.1177/1464700113499853.

Schouten, A. P., Valkenburg, P. M., & Peter, J. (2007). Precursors and underlying processes of adolescents' online self-disclosure: Developing and testing an "internet-attribute-perception" model. *Media Psychology, 10*(2), 292–315. https://doi.org/10.1080/15213260701375686.

Spooner, K., & Vaughn, M. (2016). Youth sexting: A legislative and constitutional analysis. *Journal of School Violence, 15*(2), 213–233. https://doi.org/10.1080/15388220.2014.974245.

Steinberg, L., & Morris, A. S. (2001). Adolescent development. *Journal of Cognitive Education and Psychology, 2*(1), 55–87. https://doi.org/10.1891/194589501787383444.

Steuber, K. R., & McLaren, R. M. (2015). Privacy recalibration in personal relationships: Rule usage before and after an incident of privacy turbulence. *Communication Quarterly, 63*(3), 345–364. https://doi.org/10.1080/01463373.2015.1039717.

Suler, J. (2004). The online disinhibition effect. *Cyberpsychology & Behavior, 7*(3), 321–326. https://doi.org/10.1089/1094931041291295.

Temple, J. R. (2015). A primer on teen sexting. *JAACAP Connect, 2*(4), 6–8.

Van Ouytsel, J., Van Gool, E., Walrave, M., Ponnet, K., & Peeters, E. (2016). Sexting: Adolescents' perceptions of the applications used for, motives for, and consequences of sexting. *Journal of Youth Studies*, 1–25. https://doi.org/10.1080/13676261.2016.1241865.

Van Royen, K., Poels, K., Vandebosch, H., & Adam, P. (2017). "Thinking before posting?" Reducing cyber harassment on social networking sites through a reflective message. *Computers in Human Behavior, 66*, 345–352. https://doi.org/10.1016/j.chb.2016.09.040.

Walrave, M., Vanwesenbeeck, I., & Heirman, W. (2012). Connecting and protecting? Comparing predictors of self-disclosure and privacy settings use between adolescents and adults. *Cyberpsychology: Journal of Psychosocial Research on Cyberspace, 6*(1). https://doi.org/10.5817/CP2012-1-3.

Westin, A. (1970). *Privacy and freedom*. New York: Atheneum.

CHAPTER 2

Information Disclosure, Trust and Health Risks in Online Dating

Lara Hallam, Michel Walrave,
and Charlotte J. S. De Backer

Abstract Online dating is characterized by computer-mediated communication (CMC) with a lessened availability of physical context cues, limiting online daters to nonverbally express themselves. This restricted amount of available cues generated a scientific research tension between the cues-filtered-in approach and the cues-filtered-out approach. Both theories were developed for CMC environments, yet only some explain self-disclosure and romantic relationship development in online dating. Next, the fact that online dating is initiated through CMC also encompasses enlarged opportunities of online dating profile manipulation. These different forms of deception can potentially harm online daters' mental and physical health. This chapter gives an in-depth view on all the aforementioned aspects of online dating and will further discuss interpersonal trust development through self-disclosure.

Keywords Online dating • Romantic relations • Cues-filtered-in approach • Cues-filtered-out approach

L. Hallam (✉) • M. Walrave • C. J. S. De Backer
Department of Communication Studies, MIOS, University of Antwerp,
Antwerp, Belgium

© The Author(s) 2018
M. Walrave et al. (eds.), *Sexting*, Palgrave Studies in Cyberpsychology,
https://doi.org/10.1007/978-3-319-71882-8_2

19

INTRODUCTION

In 1993, a cartoon was published in The New Yorker stating 'On the Internet, nobody knows you're a dog' (Steiner, 1993). Two decades later, while online dating sites are flourishing in our current society, the Internet is still a fairly anonymous environment (Bargh, McKenna, & Fitzsimons, 2002), where individuals can choose to hide (parts of) their entire identity online (Suler, 2004). Nevertheless, online dating has come a long way since its introduction in the 20th century with the upsurge of the Internet (Best & Delmege, 2012), and although online dating has evolved through technological changes the essence of online dating remains the same. Dating in online environments is characterized by computer-mediated communication (CMC) with less availability of nonverbal and physical context cues (Gibbs, Ellison, & Lai, 2011). CMC is synchronous (e.g., instant messaging) and/or asynchronous (e.g., email) communication, where senders encode textual messages which are sent from the senders' computers to the receivers' (Walther, 1992). Theoretically speaking, the key difference between CMC and face-to-face (FtF) communication is that it reduces nonverbal cues which are generally rich in relational information (Walther, 1992). According to Walther (2007), important impression formation features such as physical appearance or voice are often unavailable in initial CMC interactions. With regard to online dating, this means that online daters are limited in their means to nonverbally express themselves. Research on the interpersonal effects (e.g., self-disclosure or relationship development) of this restricted amount of available cues can be traced back to earlier studies about CMC contexts. Prior CMC theories such as the *lack of social context cues* (Sproull & Kiesler, 1986) predominantly viewed CMC as less rich than FtF communication. These earlier theories which fall under the overarching cues-filtered-out approach have more recently been countered by theories such as the *social information processing theory* (Walther, 1992) and *hyperpersonal communication perspective* (Walther, 1996). These theories that are part of the cues-filtered-in approach believe CMC might actually trump FtF communication in certain situations. Regardless of the amount of available nonverbal cues, online dating creates environments where interpersonal trust is developed through self-disclosure. However, the fact that online dating is initiated through CMC also enlarges opportunities of online dating deception and profile manipulation (e.g., Ellison, Hancock, & Toma, 2012; Guadagno, Okdie, & Kruse, 2012; Rege, 2009). Individuals can be deceptive by, for instance, disclosing false information about their age, physical appearance, job, income, or even relationship status (e.g., Blackhart, Fitzpatrick, & Williamson, 2014; Couch, Liamputtong, & Pitts, 2012; Guadagno et al., 2012; Hancock & Toma, 2009; Lawson & Leck, 2006; Lo, Hsieh, & Chiu, 2013; Toma & Hancock, 2012), or by engaging in romance scams (e.g., Rege, 2009; Whitty & Buchanan, 2012). These different forms of deception can potentially harm online daters' mental and physical health. Depending on the severity of the deception, victims can suffer from severe trust issues in commencing future online and offline relationships (Rege, 2009). This chapter will explore the tendency of the preceding CMC theories in order to explain and understand interpersonal effects in online dating, it will discuss the importance of self-disclosure to build interpersonal trust in online romantic relationships, and highlight some potential health risks of online dating.

DATING IN THE 21ST CENTURY

According to a Pew research (Smith, 2016) 15% of Americans have used an online dating site or app to pursue a romantic relationship online, and around one out of twenty married couples met their current partner through online dating (Smith & Anderson, 2016). To comprehend these numbers, one must understand the technological innovations and societal insights that aided in the existence of this additional form of dating. The precursor of online dating dates back to the 17th and 18th century when personal advertisements made their way in local newspapers (Best & Delmege, 2012). This period was crucial because people started to see the potential held by tabloids and broadsheets to serve as a supplementary medium to find a partner. People were able to place personal ads in a newspaper in which they indicated their need and search for a partner, and often also described themselves and their partner preferences. In the 1960s and 1970s, the computer was introduced and researchers quickly saw the opportunities of this novel medium (Best & Delmege, 2012). Moreover, the price of personal computers lowered whilst their speed and storage capacity improved (McKenna & Bargh, 1999). These technological improvements allowed for greater analyses and research. By implementing lengthy questionnaires into computers and analysing the data, analysts were now able to find personality and preference matches between those looking for a partner. A few decades later, the debut of the Internet opened doors in the quest of finding love in online environments

(Best & Delmege, 2012). Online dating websites became popular yet held a certain stigma (Anderson, 2005; Cali, Coleman, & Campbell, 2013). Online interpersonal relationships, for instance, were stigmatized as being 'talk show phenomena' with online daters being viewed as desperate, bored, lonely, or even as prosecutors of deviant behaviour (Anderson, 2005; Baker, 2002; Wildermuth, 2004). Research of Cali et al. in 2013 stated that whilst various individuals declared that online dating lost much of its original stigma, the online dating stigma is still palpable once compared with something more traditional such as offline dating (cited in Finkel, Eastwick, Karney, Reis, & Sprecher, 2012). More importantly, research of Wildermuth (2004) found that it were non-online daters in particular that held a negative stigma to romantic relationships formed online. Along these lines, a more recent 2016 report showed that online dating is losing much of its stigma (Smith & Anderson, 2016), yet is still viewed more positively by online daters compared to non-online daters (Smith, 2016). The transition of viewing online dating as a stigmatized practice towards a common way of dating went hand in hand with the aforementioned technological innovations. It aided in a shift in perspective from viewing CMC as a restricted form of communication towards a more comprehensive communication form which allows individuals to form interpersonal and romantic relationships online.

Explaining Interpersonal Effects of Computer Mediated Communication

The lessened availability of nonverbal cues influences users' view of the shared communication context and their perception of other online participants (Walther, 1992). In order to explain interpersonal effects such as self-disclosure and romantic relationship development in online dating, theorists have relied on prior CMC research as a source of inspiration. Interestingly, scholars have predominantly based their online dating findings on the later CMC theories related to the cues-filtered-in approach (e.g., *social information processing theory* and *hyperpersonal communication perspective*) instead of the earlier work belonging to the cues-filtered-out approach (e.g., *lack of social context cues*) due to the potential incapability of these senior theories to fully grasp and explain individuals' online dating behaviour. Below, the relevant different theoretical viewpoints which belong to the cues-filtered-in and cues-filtered-out approach will be discussed.

For instance, one of the earliest theoretical views on CMC environments is the *lack of social context cues*. According to Sproull and Kiesler (1986), the key difference between communicating FtF and CMC is the absence of several social context cues. In offline settings, communicators interpret the social context based on static (e.g., people's appearance, personal artefacts, ...) as well as dynamic cues (e.g., nonverbal behaviour such as nodding and eye contact) (Sproull & Kiesler, 1986). However, in our current society technologies are enhancing and advancing the existing CMC environments whilst creating possibilities for innovative communication structures by including other cues such as auditory, visual and audio-visual cues (Antheunis, Valkenburg, & Peter, 2010). Due to the fact that online dating cannot be separated from its Internet-based dating context and the growing availability of nonverbal cues, Sproull and Kiesler's (1986) theory falls short because their main focus doesn't really consider the contextual and functional processes (Walther, 1992). This theoretical view as well as other earlier CMC theories focused predominantly on the absence of cues in CMC environments, and were labelled by Culnan and Markus (1987) as the cues-filtered-out approach (Walther, 1992). This approach suggests that the lack of media richness of online communication restricts information exchange (Best & Delmege, 2012; Walther & Parks, 1992). When it comes to online dating, the cues-filtered-out approach does not seem to offer a reasonable explanation why people would (continue to) engage in online dating. Firstly, multiple online dating platforms try to implement technological novelties such as auditory and visual cues which enhances the supply of nonverbal cues (Antheunis et al., 2010). And secondly, if CMC would cripple our communication in such a way as previously proposed, one may wonder why the phenomenon of online dating is not yet extinct or why people still self-disclose online.

The cues-filtered-out approach was answered by a theoretical rebuttal named the cues-filtered-in approach which suggests that the online denial of nonverbal cues means that people will search for other information or cues which are available to compensate for possible absent cues (Best & Delmege, 2012, p. 243; Walther & Parks, 1992). Even though online dating environments differ in their availability of physical and nonverbal cues during the initiation and development of interpersonal relationships online, the subtracted range of cues may actually be liberating (Kang & Hoffman, 2011). This liberating feeling is caused by the stranger on the train effect (see Rubin, 1975), and makes people more willing to disclose information (McKenna, Green, & Gleason, 2002). This implies that because of the absent FtF communication barrier, Internet users such as online daters are more eager to self-disclose intimate information through images or text (Bargh et al., 2002; Gibbs et al., 2011; Gibbs, Ellison, & Heino, 2006; Suler, 2004). Under this cues-filtered-in approach falls the second, yet more recent, CMC theory. The *social information processing* (SIP) perspective looks further than the issues of initial computer-mediated contacts, and theorizes about the changes taking place when communicators keep interacting over different periods of time (Walther, 1992). Opposed to the theories covered by the cues-filtered-out approach, the SIP perspective is driven by the idea that CMC users want to create social relationships (Walther, 1996). According to Walther (1992), CMC users have certain drives or relational motivators which guide them to form impressions solely based on the available amount of cues (Gibbs et al., 2006; Walther, 1992). This SIP perspective provides a framework which looks further than initial contact and attempts to specify the underlying mechanisms for understanding CMC development (Walther, 1992). The SIP theory has been a source of inspiration for research, such as for instance Farrer and Gavin's (2009) work which aimed to offer an in-depth look into online dating. Furthermore, research of Gibbs et al. (2006) found support for the SIP theory in online dating by indicating that online daters also self-disclose negative personal information due to the expected face-te-face contact. In sum, SIP theory goes further than other theories and perspectives because it takes into account the anticipated future interaction by focusing on information-seeking strategies that are likely to be based on the relational goals of the users (Gibbs et al., 2006). Finally, the *hyperpersonal communication perspective* (Walther, 1996) attempts to combine media characteristics, social phenomena and other social-psychological processes by proposing a framework which believes CMC can exceed FtF interactions. According to Walther's (1996) hyperpersonal perspective, there are four types of interactions which expand our interpersonal capabilities in CMC, namely interactions of communication media with source, receiver, (asynchronous) channels, and feedback loop. Whilst the SIP perspective (Walther, 1992) looked at how CMC develops after the initial conversations, the hyperpersonal perspective aims to go one step further by analysing how CMC can even be used to one's advantage. This framework states that individuals who communicate online can 'exploit the capabilities of text-based, nonvisual interaction to form levels of affinity that would be unexpected in offline interactions' (Walther, Slovacek, & Tidwell, 2001, p. 110). Due to the absence of physical appearance or behavioural cues, other communication components are highlighted and CMC users develop personal skills to interpret the intended communication which are sent through textual messages (Kang & Hoffman, 2011; Walther, 2007). The hyperpersonal communication perspective has been applied by Toma, Hancock, and Ellison (2008) in the context of online dating by stating that compared to offline daters, online daters deliberately and strategically plan, create, and edit their self-presentation as well as their messages in order to maximize the interaction goals.

All the previously mentioned theories and perspectives start from the dominant view that individuals interact with each other in CMC environments which are typified by less physical context cues and dyadic communication (Antheunis et al., 2010). However, only the latter theories of the cues-filtered-in approach have been used to explain interpersonal effects in online dating. These theories believe that CMC opens a wide range of opportunities regarding self-disclosure due to the anticipated future interactions (Gibbs et al., 2006) and the disinhibition effect which in its turn can result in interpersonal trust and romantic relationships (Altman & Taylor, 1973; McKenna & Bargh, 1999).

Online Romantic Relationship Development Through Self-Disclosure

One of the premises of developing a romantic relationship online is that individuals are being faced with new challenges regarding self-presentation and self-disclosure (Gibbs et al., 2006). Previous research about traditional offline settings defined self-disclosure as acknowledging personal information about oneself (Derlega, Metts, Petronio, & Margulis, 1993; Schouten, Valkenburg, & Peter, 2015). Disclosing personal information in FtF settings has proven to play an important role for initiating relationships (Altman & Taylor, 1973; Derlega et al., 1993; Hollenbaugh & Everett, 2013) as well as for forming initial impressions of the communication partners (Berger & Calabrese, 1975). Yet, even though some of the self-presentational strategies that people employ are in certain aspects similar to offline meetings, one cannot get past the fact that in CMC environments individuals have different opportunities for presenting themselves (Gibbs et al., 2006). More specifically, the social cues potentially hidden behind the digital curtain of anonymity (Cheshire, 2011) and the opportunity for asynchronous communication in CMC contexts are two crucial aspects influencing individuals' self-disclosure and self-presentation

(Gibbs et al., 2006). The idea that people are engaging in a partially anonymous context allows them to take on different personas whilst expressing themselves freely (Bargh et al., 2002; Suler, 2004). The disinhibition to express oneself candidly whilst disclosing personal information in an anonymous CMC context is the result of CMC users' exemption of others' expectations and constraints (Bargh et al., 2002; McKenna et al., 2002; Suler, 2004). The self-disclosure which happens in online anonymous environments contains similar characteristics as the 'stranger on the train' phenomenon (see Rubin, 1975), because neither the online communicators nor the strangers on a train have access to a person's inner circle and will probably never see each other again (Bargh et al., 2002; Derlega & Chaikin, 1977; Hollenbaugh & Everett, 2013; McKenna et al., 2002). Apart from the fact that people disclose more personal information in anonymous online environments due to this disinhibition effect, online settings also give people with fewer social skills (e.g., social anxiety) the opportunity to engage in self-disclosure which might lead to the development of intimate relationships (McKenna et al., 2002; McKenna & Bargh, 1999). McKenna et al. (2002) argue in favour of the hyperpersonal perspective (see Walther, 1996) and state that closeness and intimacy will be developed faster in online relationships due to the disinhibition to disclose intimate and personal information. Eventually, not solely intimacy but also trust is generated through the sharing of self-relevant information with (romantic) relationship partners (McKenna et al., 2002). However, it is important to note that it is not just the surrounding anonymity that facilitates intimacy, but also a person's basic capacity to form emotional connections with other people (Scott, Mottarella, & Lavooy, 2006).

Apart from weighing which intimate information to disclose to whom in online conversations, much thought and consideration also goes into the process of self-presentation in online dating environments. Online dating profiles are 'a crucial self-presentation tool because it is the first and primary means of expressing oneself during the early stages of a correspondence and can therefore foreclose or create relationship opportunities' (Ellison, Heino, & Gibbs, 2006, p. 423). So when Goffman (1959) introduced his early work on impression management, explaining how 'the world is a stage', little did he know that the best was yet to come. With current online environments, impression management reaches a new level and the choices regarding online self-presentation seem endless. Online daters' profiles are built on self-presentational choices (Hancock & Toma, 2009) where knowledge on how to display yourself is of great importance for future relational success. Whilst presenting themselves online, individuals can choose from a wide variety of multimedia content from textual (e.g., text-based self-descriptions) to visual information (e.g., photos, video recordings, ...), or by interacting with others using synchronous as well as asynchronous messaging tools (e.g., e-mail, instant messaging, ...) (Gibbs et al., 2006). A crucial difference between offline and online self-presentation is that, if wanted, the latter can be done in a more deliberate and selective manner (Gibbs et al., 2006). Online daters have more time to think about their photographs and personal information, as well as the messages they're sending out to potential partners. Thus, the computer-mediated context of online dating allows individuals to present themselves in the most positive way (Gibbs et al., 2006), or to present their 'real' selves (Bargh et al., 2002). Research has shown that online daters realize the importance of the provided information (e.g. Yurchisin, Watchravesringkan, & Mccabe, 2005), and that their self-representational choices are often guided by two underlying tensions: (1) to appear authentic and honest, and (2) to enhance their attractiveness (Hancock & Toma, 2009). An online dater's authenticity can be influenced by warrants such as the use of their real name, identifiable and clear pictures, or third-party acquaintances (e.g., friends and family) (Reinecke & Trepte, 2014; Walther & Parks, 2002). These warrants eventually link the online self with the tangible bodily self, something which is generally unquestioned and unambiguous in offline dating (Walther & Parks, 2002).

Individuals use photographs to portray their image and visualize their appearance on the one hand, but also to stress the qualities that are of importance to them on the other hand (Ellison et al., 2006; Siibak, 2015). The information and especially the photographs individuals use as a means to express who they are whilst forming their identity, play a crucial role in online environments as well as online dating. However, due to the fact that photographs can be staged, it is difficult to estimate whether the photos represent individuals' behaviours or themselves (Siibak, 2015). Research of Ellison et al. (2006) states that individuals' photo selection is a conscious process in which the represented behaviours and poses are according to a 'set of rules' (Siibak, 2015). Even though photographs are important in all online settings, they take on a more distinctive role in online dating because of the anticipated FtF interaction (Ellison et al., 2006; Gibbs et al., 2006). According to Hancock and Toma (2009), the profile picture is a key component of online self-presentation, and what's more, it is also crucial for relational success because men as well as women are more likely to view online dating profiles containing a photograph compared to profiles that do not. Thus, whilst photos are used for impression management during profile construction on the one hand, they are also used as a means to attract other Internet users or online daters. Prior research indicated that individuals cannot overcome the fact that it is crucial to represent oneself in a physically favourable manner even in online settings which were actually considered to be faceless environments, such as social network sites and dating websites (Siibak, 2015). The underlying choice for profile photos is driven by an attempt to present an authentic self, whilst distinctly stressing one's own desirability (Ward, 2016). Moreover, presenting oneself in a physically attractive manner can nourish the development of an individual's *sexual* self. The sexual self-concept is 'considered a multidimensional construct that refers to an individual's positive and negative perceptions and feelings about him- or herself as a sexual being' (Rostosky, Dekhtyar, Cupp, & Anderman, 2008, p. 277). This sexual self-concept refers to 'an individual's evaluation of his/her own sexual thoughts, feelings, and actions' (Winter, 1988, p. 124). Breakwell and Millward (1997) argued that the sexual self-concept, being the outcome of personal experiences and social representational influences, plays a pivotal role which motivates individuals' decision for their choice of sexual risk-taking (e.g., multiple partnering, sex without condoms, or -considering a more contemporary time setting- also sexting). The more contemporary sexual behaviour of sexting (i.e., the sending of self-made sexually explicit pictures, or the sending of self-made sexually texts *and* pictures) is a well-studied phenomenon (Benotsch, Snipes, Martin, & Bull, 2013; Mitchell, Finkelhor, Jones, & Wolak, 2012; Van Ouytsel, Walrave, Ponnet, & Heirman, 2015; Walrave, Heirman, & Hallam, 2014) and occurs in online environments such as social networking sites and online dating platforms. Applying the rationale that the sexual self-concept might be related to other risk-taking behaviours (Breakwell & Millward, 1997) to our current 21st century dating scene, one may argue that an individuals' sexual self might drive contemporary behaviours such as sending sexually explicit photographs or images to others.

Interpersonal Online Trust Through Self-Disclosure

Whilst the premise of online dating is that individuals initiate online relationships with people they have never met offline, the opportunity to exploit the fairly anonymous system is on the table (Donn & Sherman, 2002; Gibbs et al., 2011). As a consequence, an intricate situation occurs with on the one hand people becoming more aware and cautious of the information they disclose online and to whom they disclose this information (Gibbs et al., 2011), and needing self-disclosure to reduce uncertainty (Antheunis, Schouten, Valkenburg, & Peter, 2012) and verify online credibility of other CMC users on the other hand (Gibbs et al., 2011). Prior research investigated and identified uncertainty reduction strategies (Berger & Calabrese, 1975; Tidwell & Walther, 2002) within the field of social networking (e.g., Antheunis et al., 2010, 2012; Gibbs et al., 2011). Individuals have used passive, active and interactive strategies to tackle potential risks and feelings of uncertainty (Antheunis et al., 2010, 2012; Berger & Calabrese, 1975; Gibbs et al., 2011; Tidwell & Walther, 2002).

Research regarding online dating found that online daters gather information in online as well as offline domains about potential partners to reduce potential uncertainty (Gibbs et al., 2011). Moreover, online daters' uncertainty reduction behaviour is predicted by three sets of privacy-related concerns (i.e., personal security, misrepresentation, and recognition), and also by self-efficacy (Gibbs et al., 2011). According to Gibbs et al. (2011) the privacy risks ingrained in online dating (e.g., identity theft, stalking, photo recognition by unintended audiences, deception or misrepresentation) in combination with the pressure to self-disclose personal information to form potential romantic relationships, are likely to inspire uncertainty reducing behaviours which are aimed at verifying potential partners' credibility. They state that because the underlying idea and pivotal goal of online dating is to find a potential romantic partner, online daters are inclined to use interactive strategies by directly engaging with others to verify self-disclosed personal information. Research showed that even though online daters prefer interactive strategies, they also tend to use other information-seeking strategies to authenticate others' identity claims by seeking out third-party information with high warranting value, such as checking public records or using Google (Gibbs et al., 2011). In sum, online daters are incentivized to verify identity claims in order to become less vulnerable themselves (Gibbs et al., 2011).

Apart from the privacy concerns mentioned by Gibbs et al. (2011), there are also legitimate trust concerns about meeting (potentially harmful) others in a shared Internet context (Cheshire, 2011; Donn & Sherman, 2002). In an online context, individuals cannot carelessly rely on the social cues used for risk and uncertainty detection (Cheshire, 2011). Nonetheless, in the development of romantic relationships, trust is the groundwork for developing interpersonal relationships (e.g., Larzelere & Huston, 1980). Prior to discussing the impact and importance of trust, it is important to state and elaborate on the difference between trust and trustworthiness. Trust and trustworthiness are two interwoven concepts, yet are distinctively different from each other (Toma, 2010). On the one hand, trust is an action of the trustor and is defined as 'the expectations that others (i.e., the trustees) will perform a certain action important to the trustor in environments characterized by uncertainty and informational incompleteness' (Toma, 2010, p. 14). According to Toma (2010), the prerequisites for trust are (1) the presence of risk when there are unknown motives of the trustees, and (2) the trustor's vulnerability. Trustworthiness, on the other hand, is 'a characteristic of the trustee that indicates he or she is worthy of trust' (Toma, 2010, p. 14). Whilst perceiving an individual as trustworthy is more the one-sided view of the trustor that can be done by examining someone's static profile information, the development of interpersonal trust is an interactive process between trustor and trustee (Toma, 2010).

Trust helps us in the decision making process of whether we should interact with a specific person in a specific context or not, and is needed in order for people to disclose more about themselves (Rosen, Cheever, Cummings, & Felt, 2008). McKenna et al. (2002) state that the establishment of trust and liking between relationship partners is a prerequisite to disclose quite intimate information about oneself. By the same token, the reciprocity of self-disclosure is thus based on the reciprocity of trust (Altman & Taylor, 1973; Larzelere & Huston, 1980). With online relationships, however, the formation of reciprocal trust and the disclosure of intimate information (e.g., personal textual and visual information), happens over the width of the Internet. In this popular form of Internet communication, trust is inherent to all components of the user experience throughout the online dating trajectory, such as online messaging, telephone conversations and eventually FtF interactions (Cheshire, 2011). Because apart from being an additional means to find a potential partner and build a romantic relationship, online dating offers the opportunity to build online trust over time through various communication forms (Cheshire, 2011). In order to establish interpersonal trust, the communicators must self-disclose personal information to each other in a reciprocal manner. It comes to no surprise that in online dating and other online environments Internet users expect others to not abuse the self-disclosed personal information. Individuals will not disclose personal information unless they have formed a dyadic boundary ensuring no leakages of the shared information (Derlega & Chaikin, 1977; McKenna et al., 2002). Previous research has studied the relationship between trust and self-disclosure in the form of textual (i.e.., text messages, emails, iMessage, ...) and visual information (i.e...., multimedia messages, sexting, ...) (e.g., Hasinoff & Shepherd, 2014; Peterson-Iyer, 2013; Zemmels & Khey, 2015). These authors state that individuals' reputation depend on whom they choose to trust with the disclosed private digital content (Hasinoff & Shepherd, 2014), and that a high trust level is needed between partners in order for emotional intimacy to be sincere (Peterson-Iyer, 2013). In later stages of the online dating trajectory, the self-disclosed information can be used for harmful causes ranging from identity theft to distribution of your sent sexts. For instance, one of the risks of sexting without the presence of interpersonal trust is that individuals depersonalize the sexualized body which leaves the nude photo to be evaluated in terms of size, shape of beauty (Peterson-Iyer, 2013). In conclusion, even though the entire online dating trajectory starts out with highly uncertain but low-risk inter-actions, they can quickly expand to online as well as offline situations where physical, personal and emotional risks are more numerous (Cheshire, 2011). However, and more importantly, when interpersonal trust is established and respected, the sharing of intimate textual and visual information can contribute to a more valuable romantic relationship.

POTENTIAL RISKS RELATED TO ONLINE DATING

In online dating, individuals can meet others with whom they build inter-personal trust by sharing personal and intimate textual and visual informa-tion, which in its turn might lead to new relationships. However, not all is rosy online. Because online dating equals meeting someone through an online platform, potential risks and deception accompany this form of dat-ing (Blackhart et al., 2014). People can be deceptive in their profiles and disclose false information about their age, physical appearance, job, income, or even relationship status (e.g., Blackhart et al., 2014; Couch et al., 2012; Guadagno et al., 2012; Hancock & Toma, 2009; Lawson & Leck, 2006; Lo et al., 2013; Toma & Hancock, 2012). As Blackhart et al. (2014, p. 114) state 'those who engage in online dating simply do not know who is on the other side of a computer'. It is the inability to verify whom we are communicating with online that can give rise to different types of risks and dangers.

Donn and Sherman (2002) state that many online daters have trust issues about meeting potentially harmful others. In the early stages of online dating whilst there was still a stigma about meeting others online, individuals feared the possibility of meeting a sexual predator or 'psycho' (Anderson, 2005; Finkel et al., 2012). Nowadays, this risk still exists, but online dating environments can set a higher threshold for membership, guaranteeing their members qualitative potential partners and creating an acceptable risk level for initiating relationships (Finkel et al., 2012). Moreover, apart from providing online dating safety tips, certain safety labels which guarantee transparency and policies against dating scams are awarded to certain online dating sites. These safety labels aim to serve as a warrant against online dating romance scams. In this relatively new type of emotionally devastating fraud, third-party scammers fake a romantic relationship through online dating and then ask for large amounts of money (Rege, 2009; Whitty & Buchanan, 2012). According to Rege (2009) this particular type of fraud thrives on the presence of a strong social bond that has generated trust between the victims and the scammer. Consequently, the pitfalls of meeting potentially harmful or deceptive others can result in emotional harm such as severe trust issues towards meeting individuals online and starting new relationships (Rege, 2009). These trust issues are not solely a result of being led astray for monetary goods, but also after other trust violations. More specifically, when online daters as well as other Internet users have engaged in sexting in online (dating) environments, the confidentiality of the pictures are in peril. In online environments that are based on mutual respect and trust, sexting can be an important part of the relationship development and of the exploration of the sexual self. However, the possible consequence of interpersonal trust violation is the unauthorized public circulation of private pictures which might influence the dignitary and emotional harm (Day, 2010).

CONCLUSION

Online dating has grown from a stigmatized phenomenon of which people thought only desperate and shy people were the members, to a common way of meeting other individuals. As with offline dating, online daters tend to use self-disclosure to share personal information and photographs in order to form meaningful relationships that are built on interpersonal trust. While the development of this interpersonal trust was first doubted through early CMC theories such as the lack of social context cues, other theories quickly realized the potential that is held by online dating. The social information processing theory and hyperpersonal communication perspective identified the absence of nonverbal context cues as a disinhibition trigger that frees people of presumptions and judgements, and allows them to self-disclose more eagerly. This disinhibition effect results in online daters sharing intimate textual and visual information with people they've met online. Even though potential deceivers may use your personal information in possible identity fraud or forward intimate nude or semi-nude pictures to others, online dating is still booming. It allows individuals to choose partners from an enlarged pool whilst also coming up with policies and labels to ensure safe online dating.

REFERENCES

Altman, I., & Taylor, D. A. (1973). *Social penetration: The development of interpersonal relationships.* New York: Holt, Rinehart and Winston.

Anderson, T. L. (2005). Relationships among internet attitudes, internet use, romantic beliefs, and perceptions of online romantic relationships. *Cyberpsychology & Behavior, 8*(6), 521–531.

Antheunis, M. L., Schouten, A. P., Valkenburg, P. M., & Peter, J. (2012). Interactive uncertainty reduction strategies and verbal affection in computer-mediated communication. *Communication Research, 39*(6), 757–780. https://doi.org/10.1177/0093650211410420.

Antheunis, M. L., Valkenburg, P. M., & Peter, J. (2010). Getting acquainted through social network sites: Testing a model of online uncertainty reduction and social attraction. *Computers in Human Behavior, 26*(1), 100–109. https://doi.org/10.1016/j.chb.2009.07.005.

Baker, A. (2002). What makes an online relationship successful? Clues from couples who met in cyberspace. *Cyberpsychology & Behavior, 5*(4), 363–375. https://doi.org/10.1089/109493102760275617.

Bargh, J. A., McKenna, K. Y. A., & Fitzsimons, G. M. (2002). Can you see the real me? Activation and expression of the "true self" on the internet. *Journal of Social Issues, 58*(1), 33–48. https://doi.org/10.1111/1540-4560.00247.

Benotsch, E. G., Snipes, D. J., Martin, A. M., & Bull, S. S. (2013). Sexting, substance use, and sexual risk behavior in young adults. *Journal of Adolescent Health, 52*(3), 307–313. https://doi.org/10.1016/j.jadohealth.2012.06.011.

Berger, C. R., & Calabrese, R. J. (1975). Some explorations in initial interaction and beyond: Toward a developmental theory of interpersonal communication. *Human Communication Research, 1*(2), 99–112. https://doi.org/10.1111/j.1468-2958.1975.tb00258.x.

Best, K., & Delmege, S. (2012). The filtered encounter: Online dating and the problem of filtering through excessive information. *Social Semiotics, 22*(3), 237. https://doi.org/10.1080/10350330.2011.648405.

Blackhart, G. C., Fitzpatrick, J., & Williamson, J. (2014). Dispositional factors predicting use of online dating sites and behaviors related to online dating. *Computers in Human Behavior, 33*, 113–118. https://doi.org/10.1016/j.chb.2014.01.022.

Breakwell, G. M., & Millward, L. J. (1997). Sexual self-concept and sexual risk-taking. *Journal of Adolescence, 20*(1), 29–41. https://doi.org/10.1006/jado.1996.0062.

Cali, B. E., Coleman, J. M., & Campbell, C. (2013). Stranger danger? women's self-protection intent and the continuing stigma of online dating. *Cyberpsychology Behavior and Social Networking, 16*(12), 853–857. https://doi.org/10.1089/cyber.2012.0512.

Cheshire, C. (2011). Online trust, trustworthiness, or assurance? *Daedalus, 140*(4), 49–58. https://doi.org/10.1162/DAED_a_00114.

Couch, D., Liamputtong, P., & Pitts, M. (2012). What are the real and perceived risks and dangers of online dating? Perspectives from online daters. *Health, Risk & Society, 14*(7–8), 697–714. https://doi.org/10.1080/13698575.2012.720964.

Culnan, M. J., & Markus, M. L. (1987). Information technologies. In F. M. Jablin, L. L. Putnam, K. H. Robets, & L. W. Porter (Eds.), *Handbook of organizational communication: An interdisciplinary perspective* (pp. 420–443). Newbury Park, CA: Sage.

Day, T. (2010). The new digital dating behavior – Sexting: Teens' explicit love letters: Criminal justice or civil liability. *Hastings Communications and Entertainment Law Journal, 33*(1), 1–31. Available at SSRN: https://ssrn.com/abstract=2512409

Derlega, V. J., & Chaikin, A. L. (1977). Privacy and self-disclosure in social relationships. *Journal of Social Issues, 33*(3), 102–115. https://doi.org/10.1111/j.1540-4560.1977.tb01885.x.

Derlega, V. J., Metts, S., Petronio, S., & Margulis, S. T. (1993). *Self-disclosure*. Newbury Park, CA: Sage.

Donn, J. E., & Sherman, R. C. (2002). Attitudes and practices regarding the formation of romantic relationships on the internet. *Cyberpsychology & Behavior, 5*(2), 107–123. https://doi.org/10.1089/109493102753770499.

Ellison, N., Heino, R., & Gibbs, J. (2006). Managing impressions online: Self-presentation processes in the online dating environment. *Journal of Computer-Mediated Communication, 11*(2), 415–441. https://doi.org/10.1111/j.1083-6101.2006.00020.x.

Ellison, N. B., Hancock, J. T., & Toma, C. L. (2012). Profile as promise: A framework for conceptualizing veracity in online dating self-presentations. *New Media & Society, 14*(1), 45–62. https://doi.org/10.1177/1461444811410395.

Farrer, J., & Gavin, J. (2009). Online dating in Japan: A test of social information processing theory. *Cyberpsychology & Behavior, 12*(4), 407–412. https://doi.org/10.1089/cpb.2009.0069.

Finkel, E. J., Eastwick, P. W., Karney, B. R., Reis, H. T., & Sprecher, S. (2012). Online dating a critical analysis from the perspective of psychological science. *Psychological Science in the Public Interest, 13*(1), 3–66. https://doi.org/10.1177/1529100612436522.

Gibbs, J. L., Ellison, N. B., & Heino, R. D. (2006). Self-presentation in online personals the role of anticipated future interaction, self-disclosure, and perceived success in internet dating. *Communication Research, 33*(2), 152–177. https://doi.org/10.1177/0093650205285368.

Gibbs, J. L., Ellison, N. B., & Lai, C.-H. (2011). First comes love, then comes Google: An investigation of uncertainty reduction strategies and self-disclosure in online dating. *Communication Research, 38*(1), 70–100. https://doi.org/10.1177/0093650210377091.

Goffman, E. (1959). *The presentation of self in everyday life* (1st ed.). New York: Anchor.

Guadagno, R. E., Okdie, B. M., & Kruse, S. A. (2012). Dating deception: Gender, online dating, and exaggerated self-presentation. *Computers in Human Behavior, 28*(2), 642–647. https://doi.org/10.1016/j.chb.2011.11.010.

Hancock, J. T., & Toma, C. L. (2009). Putting your best face forward: The accuracy of online dating photographs. *Journal of Communication, 59*(2), 367–386. https://doi.org/10.1111/j.1460-2466.2009.01420.x.

Hasinoff, A. A., & Shepherd, T. (2014). Sexting in context: Privacy norms and expectations. *International Journal of Communication, 8*(0), 24.

Hollenbaugh, E. E., & Everett, M. K. (2013). The effects of anonymity on self-disclosure in blogs: An application of the online disinhibition effect. *Journal of Computer-Mediated Communication, 18*(3), 283–302. https://doi.org/10.1111/jcc4.12008.

Kang, T., & Hoffman, L. H. (2011). Why would you decide to use an online dating site? Factors that lead to online dating. *Communication Research Reports, 28*(3), 205–213. https://doi.org/10.1080/08824096.2011.566109.

Larzelere, R. E., & Huston, T. L. (1980). The dyadic trust scale: Toward understanding interpersonal trust in close relationships. *Journal of Marriage and Family, 42*(3), 595–604. https://doi.org/10.2307/351903.

Lawson, H. M., & Leck, K. (2006). Dynamics of internet dating. *Social Science Computer Review, 24*(2), 189–208. https://doi.org/10.1177/0894439305283402.

Lo, S.-K., Hsieh, A.-Y., & Chiu, Y.-P. (2013). Contradictory deceptive behavior in online dating. *Computers in Human Behavior, 29*(4), 1755–1762. https://doi.org/10.1016/j.chb.2013.02.010.

McKenna, K. Y. A., & Bargh, J. A. (1999). Causes and consequences of social interaction on the internet: A conceptual framework. *Media Psychology, 1*(3), 249–269. https://doi.org/10.1207/s1532785xmep0103_4.

McKenna, K. Y. A., Green, A. S., & Gleason, M. E. J. (2002). Relationship formation on the internet: What's the big attraction? *Journal of Social Issues, 58*(1), 9–31. https://doi.org/10.1111/1540-4560.00246.

Mitchell, K. J., Finkelhor, D., Jones, L. M., & Wolak, J. (2012). Prevalence and characteristics of youth sexting: A national study. *Pediatrics, 129*(1), 13–20. https://doi.org/10.1542/peds.2011-1730.

Peterson-Iyer, K. (2013). Mobile porn?: Teenage sexting and justice for women. *Journal of the Society of Christian Ethics, 33*(2), 93–110. https://doi.org/10.1353/sce.2013.0036.

Rege, A. (2009). What's love got to do with it? Exploring online dating scams and identity fraud. *International Journal of Cyber Criminology, 3*(2), 494.

Reinecke, L., & Trepte, S. (2014). Authenticity and well-being on social network sites: A two-wave longitudinal study on the effects of online authenticity and the positivity bias in SNS communication. *Computers in Human Behavior, 30*, 95–102. https://doi.org/10.1016/j.chb.2013.07.030.

Rosen, L. D., Cheever, N. A., Cummings, C., & Felt, J. (2008). The impact of emotionality and self-disclosure on online dating versus traditional dating. *Computers in Human Behavior, 24*(5), 2124–2157. https://doi.org/10.1016/j.chb.2007.10.003.

Rostosky, S. S., Dekhtyar, O., Cupp, P. K., & Anderman, E. M. (2008). Sexual self-concept and sexual self-efficacy in adolescents: A possible clue to promoting sexual health? *Journal of Sex Research, 45*(3), 277–286. https://doi.org/10.1080/00224490802204480.

Rubin, Z. (1975). Disclosing oneself to a stranger: Reciprocity and its limits. *Journal of Experimental Social Psychology, 11*(3), 233–260. https://doi.org/10.1016/S0022-1031(75)80025-4.

Schouten, A. P., Valkenburg, P. M., & Peter, J. (2015). An experimental test of processes underlying self-disclosure in computer-mediated communication. *Cyberpsychology: Journal of Psychosocial Research on Cyberspace, 3*(2). Retrieved from https://journals.muni.cz/cyberpsychology/article/view/4227

Scott, V. M., Mottarella, K. E., & Lavooy, M. J. (2006). Does virtual intimacy exist? A brief exploration into reported levels of intimacy in online relationships. *Cyberpsychology & Behavior: The Impact of the Internet, Multimedia and Virtual Reality on Behavior and Society, 9*(6), 759–761. https://doi.org/10.1089/cpb.2006.9.759.

Siibak, A. (2015). Constructing the self through the photo selection – Visual impression management on social networking websites. *Cyberpsychology: Journal of Psychosocial Research on Cyberspace, 3*(1) Retrieved from https://journals.muni.cz/cyberpsychology/article/view/4218

Smith, A. (2016). *15% of American adults have used online dating sites or mobile dating apps*. Washington, DC: Pew Internet.

Smith, A., & Anderson, M. (2016). *5 facts about online dating*. Washington, DC: Pew Research Center.

Sproull, L., & Kiesler, S. (1986). Reducing social context cues: Electronic mail in organizational communication. *Management Science, 32*(11), 1492–1512. https://doi.org/10.1287/mnsc.32.11.1492.

Steiner, P. (1993, July 5). On the internet, nobody knows you're a dog. *The New Yorker*, p. 61.

Suler, J. (2004). The online disinhibition effect. *Cyberpsychology & Behavior, 7*(3), 321–326. https://doi.org/10.1089/1094931041291295.

Tidwell, L. C., & Walther, J. B. (2002). Computer-mediated communication effects on disclosure, impressions, and interpersonal evaluations: Getting to know one another a bit at a time. *Human Communication Research, 28*(3), 317–348. https://doi.org/10.1111/j.1468-2958.2002.tb00811.x.

Toma, C. L. (2010). *Perceptions of trustworthiness online: The role of visual and textual information*. Presented at the CSCW '10 Proceedings of the 2010 ACM conference on computer supported cooperative work (pp. 13–22). New York: ACM. https://doi.org/10.1145/1718918.1718923.

Toma, C. L., & Hancock, J. T. (2012). What lies beneath: The linguistic traces of deception in online dating profiles. *Journal of Communication, 62*(1), 78–97. https://doi.org/10.1111/j.1460-2466.2011.01619.x.

Toma, C. L., Hancock, J. T., & Ellison, N. B. (2008). Separating fact from fiction: An examination of deceptive self-presentation in online dating profiles. *Personality and Social Psychology Bulletin, 34*(8), 1023–1036. https://doi.org/10.1177/0146167208318067.

Van Ouytsel, J., Walrave, M., Ponnet, K., & Heirman, W. (2015). The association between adolescent sexting, psychosocial difficulties, and risk behavior: Integrative review. *The Journal of School Nursing, 31*(1), 54–69. https://doi.org/10.1177/1059840514541964.

Walrave, M., Heirman, W., & Hallam, L. (2014). Under pressure to sext? Applying the theory of planned behaviour to adolescent sexting. *Behaviour & Information Technology, 33*(1), 86–98. https://doi.org/10.1080/0144929X.2013.837099.

Walther, J. B. (1992). Interpersonal effects in computer-mediated interaction a relational perspective. *Communication Research, 19*(1), 52–90. https://doi.org/10.1177/009365092019001003.

Walther, J. B. (1996). Computer-mediated communication impersonal, interpersonal, and hyperpersonal interaction. *Communication Research, 23*(1), 3–43. https://doi.org/10.1177/009365096023001001.

Walther, J. B. (2007). Selective self-presentation in computer-mediated communication: Hyperpersonal dimensions of technology, language, and cognition. *Computers in Human Behavior, 23*(5), 2538–2557. https://doi.org/10.1016/j.chb.2006.05.002.

Walther, J. B., & Parks, M. R. (1992). Relational communication in computer-mediated interaction. *Human Communication Research, 19*, 50–88.

Walther, J. B., & Parks, M. R. (2002). Cues filtered out, cues filtered in: Computer-mediated communication and relationships. In M. L. Knapp & J. A. Daly (Eds.), *Handbook of interpersonal communication* (3rd ed., pp. 529–563). Thousand Oaks, CA: SAGE.

Walther, J. B., Slovacek, C. L., & Tidwell, L. C. (2001). Is a picture worth a thousand words? Photographic images in long-term and short-term computer-mediated communication. *Communication Research, 28*(1), 105–134. https://doi.org/10.1177/009365001028001004.

Ward, J. (2016). What are you doing on tinder? Impression management on a matchmaking mobile app. *Information, Communication & Society, 20*(11), 1644–1659. Retrieved from http://www.tandfonline.com/eprint/P7Y6eb NxiMpCXvrIktYk/full

Whitty, M. T., & Buchanan, T. (2012). The online romance scam: A serious cyber-crime. *Cyberpsychology, Behavior, and Social Networking, 15*(3), 181–183. https://doi.org/10.1089/cyber.2011.0352.

Wildermuth, S. M. (2004). The effects of stigmatizing discourse on the quality of on-line relationships. *Cyberpsychology & Behavior, 7*(1), 73–84. https://doi.org/10.1089/109493104322820147.

Winter, L. (1988). The role of sexual self-concept in the use of contraceptives. *Family Planning Perspectives, 20*(3), 123–127. https://doi.org/10.2307/2135700.

Yurchisin, J., Watchravesringkan, K., & Mccabe, D. B. (2005). An exploration of identity re-creation in the context of internet dating. *Social Behavior and Personality: An International Journal, 33*(8), 735–750. https://doi.org/10.2224/sbp.2005.33.8.735.

Zemmels, D. R., & Khey, D. N. (2015). Sharing of digital visual media: Privacy concerns and trust among young people. *American Journal of Criminal Justice, 40*(2), 285–302. https://doi.org/10.1007/s12103-014-9245-7.

CHAPTER 3

A Nuanced Account: Why Do Individuals Engage in Sexting?

Joris Van Ouytsel, Michel Walrave, and Koen Ponnet

Abstract Based on a review of both quantitative and qualitative studies, this chapter aims to explore individuals' motives for engaging in sexting. The chapter outlines adolescents' and adults' various reasons for engaging in sexting, both inside and outside the context of a romantic relationship. These reasons include flirting with a date and sustaining intimacy within an already established romantic relationship. The chapter also focuses on the pressure that often accompanies sexting. Finally, the chapter discusses the potentially positive effects of exchanging sexually explicit pictures.

Keywords Sexting • Romantic relationship • Attachment • Peer pressure • Media socialization

J. Van Ouytsel (✉) • M. Walrave
Department of Communication Studies, MIOS, University of Antwerp,
Antwerp, Belgium

K. Ponnet
Department of Communication Studies, MIOS, University of Antwerp,
Antwerp, Belgium

Department of Communication Sciences, IMEC-MICT, Ghent University,
Ghent, Belgium

© The Author(s) 2018   39
M. Walrave et al. (eds.), *Sexting*, Palgrave Studies in Cyberpsychology,
https://doi.org/10.1007/978-3-319-71882-8_3

Introduction

Humans have always tended to create sexually explicit images, ranging from nude drawings to images created with a Polaroid camera. Smartphones make the creation of these images more convenient and accessible. Several scholars have argued that, in this light, sexting can be regarded as a digital extension of previous generations' exchanges of sexually explicit content using physical media, as in the sharing of written notes, photographs, or drawings (Chalfen, 2009; Curnutt, 2012; Livingstone & Görzig, 2012). Indeed, there are anecdotal accounts of private individuals using Polaroid cameras to create self-made sexually explicit images. Such instant cameras provided private users with an easy way to access their images without having to develop film at commercial laboratories (Edgley & Kiser, 1982). Anecdotal accounts (documented by Edgley & Kiser, 1982) have shown that couples used these self-made sexually explicit Polaroid photographs to enhance sexual intimacy within their romantic relationships. Couples also mailed such photographs to each other during times of separation (e.g., during trips or within long-distance relationships), and swinger couples used them to get in touch with each other (Edgley & Kiser, 1982). Sexting may be a modern extension of this behaviour, but it differs in that the potential consequences and audiences are vastly different. When compared to analogue photographs, digital photographs—even those that are meant to remain private—can be stored, reproduced, and disseminated across a wider audience and on a larger scale (Chalfen, 2009; Curnutt, 2012).

From early on, researchers on sexting among adolescents and adults have been fascinated with individuals' motives for exchanging self-made sexually explicit photographs. Lenhart (2009) conducted one of the earliest studies on the topic at the Pew Research Centre through focus-group interviews. The many subsequent studies have used a variety of methodologies and theoretical frameworks. This chapter aims to review adolescents' and adults' reasons for creating and sending self-made sexually explicit photographs. As our review will show, several of the motives that Edgley and Kiser (1982) described are still valid for modern sexting behaviours.

Sexting Within the Context of a Romantic Relationship

Adolescents' main motives for engaging in sexting include the pursuit of a romantic relationship and the desire to please an existing romantic partner. Qualitative studies have consistently found that adolescents share self-made sexually explicit photographs with their dating or romantic partners. In a retrospective study, Strohmaier, Murphy, and DeMatteo (2014) asked college students about their sexting experiences as minors and found that sexting within the context of a romantic relationship and flirting with potential romantic partners were the most important factors for engaging in sexting. As Le, Temple, Peskin, Markham, and Tortolero (2014) argued, sexting can—through the technological features that provide creators with ways to craft images and responses—provide teenagers with a "more removed and disinhibiting form of flirtation" (Le et al., 2014, p. 70). During times of physical separation, such as often occur in long-distance relationships, partners can use sexting to remain sexually engaged (Walker, Sanci, & Temple-Smith, 2013). In a study of college students, Drouin, Vogel, Surbey, and Stills (2013) found that a quarter of those who engaged in sexting with romantic partners did so because their partners were far away. For others, sexting was a way to express their sexuality even when religious rules and practices prohibited them from doing so in physical ways (Lippman & Campbell, 2014).

However, although sexting can be a consensual form of intimate communication within romantic relationships, individuals can also be pressured to engage in sexting. A study of US adolescents found that female teenagers who experienced sexual coercion were more likely to engage in sexting. More particularly, offline sexual coercion was positively associated with being asked for sexually explicit images, actually sending those images, and receiving unsolicited sexting messages (Choi, Van Ouytsel, & Temple, 2016). Therefore, some forms of sexting could be part of a broader range of sexual coercion. The intimate pictures, once sent can be used to further threaten or blackmail the victim. The Choi et al. (2016) study confirms what scholars have observed in other qualitative studies among adolescents: that some girls engage in sexting due to pressure. In both the US and the UK, researchers have observed the gender dynamics involved in the coercion of girls related to sexting (Lippman & Campbell, 2014; Ringrose, Harvey, Gill, & Livingstone, 2013; Walker et al., 2013). Girls can be simultaneously pressured into sexting and criticized if they do engage in such behaviour. This indicates a double standard in relation to sexting. Which means that girls and boys are judged differently for the same behaviour (Lippman & Campbell, 2014). Although girls are pressured to engage in sexting, boys are pressured (typically by male peers) to share the explicit images that they receive from girls. Some boys experience criticism if they do not participate in the behaviour; for instance, some boys have been called "gay" for not collecting or for refusing to view or share girls' sexting images (Walker et al., 2013).

Another study (Englander, 2015), this one among undergraduates (18- and 19-year-olds), found that, of those who engaged in sexting, almost one third (30%) said that they did so only because they wanted to and that they were by no means pressured into it. However, one in ten participants (12%) declared that they always felt coerced when engaging in sexting. The remainder of the surveyed adolescents (58%) sometimes felt pressure to send sexually explicit pictures; in sum, 70% said that they felt some kind of pressure. Moreover, gender differences were found: Half of the male respondents but only one fourth of the female respondents declared that they always engaged in sexting voluntarily. Further, Englander (2015) found that, among subjects who reported having never engaged in voluntary sexting, that act most likely occurred in response to serious threats or intense fear. Finally, those who reported having always sexted under pressure started sexting at a younger age than did those whose sexting was totally voluntarily. This may indicate that sexting at a young age is, for at least some individuals, associated with pressure.

Regarding the sources of pressure, Englander (2015) found that those who voluntary engaged in sexting were mostly taking pictures to send to their romantic partners. By contrast, those who reported having been pressured to engage in sexting were mostly sending pictures to *potential* partners; mostly girls experienced this situation. Sexting somebody who is not a romantic partner could augment the risks of sexting exposure. Nevertheless, most of those who had voluntarily engaged in sexting reported no negative outcomes. For instance, three fourths of those who engaged in sexting reported that, to their knowledge, the recipients had kept their pictures confidential. For the remaining one fourth of those who engaged in sexting, however, peers and/or adults saw their sexually explicit pictures.

Sexting as a Bridge to Actual Sexual Behaviour

Sexting can also be a way for people, especially adolescents, to experiment with their sexuality; in this way, it can function as a first step toward the initiation of offline sexual behaviours (Drouin et al., 2013). Multiple researchers have identified sexting as being cross-sectionally associated with sexual behaviour and sexually risky behaviour (such as having sex without protection and having sex after using alcohol or drugs) among adolescents (Houck et al., 2014; Rice et al., 2014; Temple et al., 2012; Van Ouytsel, Walrave, Ponnet, & Heirman, 2015; Ybarra & Mitchell, 2014). Using a longitudinal design, which allows for behaviour to be studied for a longer period of time and for assumptions based on causality to be tested, Temple and Choi (2014) found that youths who had engaged in sexting were more likely than those who had not, to be sexually active a year later. This indicates that some youths may engage in sexting to signal to their partners that they are willing to engage in sexual behaviour or be more intimate (Temple & Choi, 2014). Houck et al. (2014) found, using a sample of at-risk early adolescents, that those who engaged in sexting had greater intention to engage in sexual activity than those who did not. Sexting therefore seems to be a first step towards actual sexual behaviour for some youth (Lenhart, 2009). From this perspective, sexting can be understood as a form of sexual exploration and experimentation as part of the development of sexual identity; these are hallmarks of the adolescent developmental period (Livingstone & Görzig, 2012). Technology could provide either a driving or a supporting role within sexual experimentation (Draper, 2011). Although there is little evidence that sexting is used in lieu of actual sexual contact, some scholars have argued that some adolescents use it as a way to practice safe sex (e.g., to avoid getting pregnant or contracting a sexually transmitted infection) or because they are not allowed to engage in physical sexual behaviours due to religious restrictions (Chalfen, 2009).

Drouin et al. (2013) found that, among college students, sexting is often used to initiate sex, especially with casual sex partners or when cheating on a relationship partner. Perkins, Becker, Tehee, and Mackelprang (2013) found that college students who engaged in sexting initiated sex at earlier ages and had more sexual partners over their lifetimes than those who did not. Sexting has also been found to be a partial mediator between problematic alcohol use and casual sexual encounters (Dir, Cyders, & Coskunpinar, 2013). Dir et al. (2013) found that alcohol use increases the likelihood that college students will engage in sexting, as it lowers inhibitions, which can lead to actual sexual behaviour.

Adults have also been found to use sexting to cheat on romantic partners (Drouin et al., 2013; Wysocki & Childers, 2011). Researchers in one study found that about half of the surveyed users of the affair website AshleyMadison.com to send nude photos of themselves over e-mail or a cell phone (Wysocki & Childers, 2011).

SEXTING AND SOCIAL PRESSURE

Individuals can feel pressure to engage in sexting from not just a romantic partner but also friends. Especially among adolescents, peer-group social norms are becoming increasingly important (Steinberg, 2011). Research has consistently found that teenagers who perceive the social norms regarding sexting as being positive are more likely to engage in that behaviour. Youths who engage in sexting may assume that it is normative among their peers (Rice et al., 2012). Houck et al. (2014) found, in a sample of at-risk early adolescents, that youths who had sent self-made sexually explicit text messages or photographs were more likely to perceive that their peers, the media, and their parents approved of that behaviour. Lee, Moak, and Walker (2016) found that youths who perceived higher peer pressure to engage in sexting were more likely to create and send self-made sexually explicit pictures or videos of themselves and of others.

When studying sexting from the perspective of the Theory of Planned Behaviour, Walrave, Heirman, and Hallam (2014) found that the perceived peer norms regarding sexting significantly predicted adolescents' intentions to send self-made sexually explicit photographs or text messages. However, the social influences on individuals' sexting behaviours can be very subtle and can extend beyond significant others' approval or disapproval of sexting. One study observed that when adolescents hold a more positive image of peers who send sexually explicit photographs, they relate more to the characteristics of such individuals and have a higher willingness to engage in sexting (Walrave et al., 2015). In other words, both significant others' opinions and the perceived image of peers who send sexting images can pressure individuals into engaging in sexting. More specifically, some researchers found that 54% of respondents in a sample knew someone who had sent a sexually explicit picture or text message via a cell phone (Rice et al., 2012). Youth who engaged in sexting were also more likely than those who did not to have peers who also engaged in the behaviours (Rice et al., 2012). Youths who associate with deviant peers (i.e., those who engage in a variety of deviant behaviours, ranging from logging into someone's e-mail or social media accounts without their permission to illegally copying music, videos, or software) have also been found to be more likely to have sent naked pictures of themselves via cell phones (Ricketts, Maloney, Marcum, & Higgins, 2015).

Sexting and Media Socialization

Sexting can also be understood from a media socialization perspective. Several scholars have hypothesized that, within the media landscape, sexualized media, such as sexually explicit music videos and pornography, are very prevalent and that such media could be an influential factor in adolescents' engagement in sexting (Chalfen, 2009, 2010; Curnutt, 2012). Similarly, celebrities are posting sexually explicit photographs on social media (e.g., Twitter or Instagram) accounts (Curnutt, 2012). However, exposure to others' sexual self-presentation (e.g., images on social networking sites that portray others with a sexual gaze or with a sexual or scantily dressed appearance) has not been found to directly influence adolescents' engagement in sexting behaviour (van Oosten & Vandenbosch, 2017; Van Ouytsel, Ponnet, Walrave, & d'Haenens, 2017). These self-presentations on social media could have an indirect impact by influencing the social norms surrounding sexting (van Oosten & Vandenbosch, 2017). Further research is needed to substantiate this hypothesis, however.

Researchers have found associations between pornography and sending sexually explicit images among both boys and girls (Romito & Beltramini, 2015; Stanley et al., 2016; Van Ouytsel, Ponnet, & Walrave, 2014). Van Ouytsel et al. (2014) found that watching music videos (which often feature sexually explicit themes) was linked with both requests for and receipt of sexting images among boys only. Van Ouystel et al. hypothesized that this relationship between sexting and music-video consumption among boys, but not among girls, could be explained by the idea that music videos are more likely to propagate sexually active roles for males and submissive roles for females. Young people might be affected by these sexual scripts, which might be reflected in their sexting behaviours. Although the associations between sexting, highly sexualized media, and consumer culture are found in empirical studies, there is no causal evidence regarding this relationship. Because of the cross-sectional nature of these studies, the associations between sexting and media use may be symptomatic of a lifestyle in which young people who frequently consume sexualized media content are more likely than those who do not to also engage in sexting behaviours.

The Positive Effects of Sexting

Although the majority of research on sexting and on participants' motivations has been focused on the potential risks of this behaviour and on its ties to abusive relationships (Choi et al., 2016; Drouin, Ross, & Tobin,

2015), some researchers have begun to look into the potentially positive effects of sexting behaviour. The evidence for the potentially positive effects on romantic relationships is mixed. The researchers in one study of adults found that sexting was cross-sectionally associated with higher perceptions of consensus within romantic relationships; this association between sexting and a component of relationship satisfaction suggests that sexting could be a part of a satisfying relationship or that it could even strengthen romantic relationships (Parker, Blackburn, Perry, & Hawks, 2012).

Moreover, qualitative research has shown that some people experience sexting as a way to communicate and facilitate sexual desires and pleasure or as a way to maintain intimacy within a romantic relationship (Burkett, 2015). Researchers have also found that consensual sexting among young adults was associated with positive relational consequences for half of the surveyed participants and negative consequences for the other half. Furthermore, the latter group experienced feelings of regret, discomfort, and even trauma following the sexting. These consequences differed by gender, relationship type, and attachment. Women, especially those in casual relationships, were more inclined to report negative consequences than positive ones. Within committed relationships, these gender differences did not appear. In general, individuals with low attachment avoidance (i.e., individuals who did not have a tendency to keep their distance from their partners) experienced more positive (relational) outcomes and fewer negative consequences when sexting (Drouin, Coupe, & Temple, 2017). Some scholars have found that sexting is only related to relationship satisfaction among men and that only women with an anxious attachment style (i.e., being afraid of losing one's partner) reported that sexting had positive outcomes on relationship satisfaction (McDaniel & Drouin, 2015). These contrasting results highlight the importance of investigating sexting within various relational contexts (e.g., committed versus casual relationships) and attachment styles. In sum, differences between couples may exist in terms of sexting expectations and attachment styles, and these differences may translate to other relational tensions. As most negative consequences have been observed in non-committed relationships, awareness of the possible negative consequences of sexting with casual partners may need to be increased (Drouin et al., 2017).

CONCLUSION

The scientific literature on sexting includes a diverse range of reasons as to why individuals exchange sexually explicit pictures of themselves. Most sexting occurs within the context of a romantic relationship and can be considered a positive experience. In the context of these romantic relationships, sexting can be used to show romantic interest, to flirt, or to sustain intimacy. In general, sexting can be a way to engage in sexual experimentation and can be associated with sexual behaviour. Based on longitudinal research, there is also evidence that sexting precedes physical sexual behaviour.

However, sexting can also occur within the context of abusive relationships and can be caused by peer pressure. Especially among adolescents, peer norms are important. Teenagers who perceived that positive peer-based social norms regarding sexting were more likely to engage in that practice. Moreover, young people are growing up in a media-centric culture. Although young people's exposure to sexual celebrity photos has not been found to directly impact adolescents' sexting, it might influence young people's social norms concerning that practice. Some scholars have linked watching pornography or music videos to sexting behaviour. Still, further research is needed to investigate these associations.

More research is also warranted regarding the potentially positive impact of sexting within romantic relationships, as the current results are mixed. Some researchers have found sexting to be related to higher perceptions of consensus between romantic partners. Moreover, sexting has been found to be a way to communicate sexual desire and to maintain intimacy. However, researchers have also found negative relational consequences for sexting participants. Therefore, it remains unclear when sexting has a positive impact on relationship quality. More research is warranted regarding sexting's impact on romantic relationships; regardless of the media through which sexting messages are exchanged, sexting behaviour is here to stay, as it reflects humans' desire to engage in the creation of sexually explicit messages and imagery.

REFERENCES

Burkett, M. (2015). Sex(t) talk: A qualitative analysis of young adults' negotiations of the pleasures and perils of sexting. *Sexuality & Culture, 19*(4), 835–863. https://doi.org/10.1007/s12119-015-9295-0.

Chalfen, R. (2009). It's only a picture': Sexting, 'smutty' snapshots and felony charges. *Visual Studies,* 24(3), 258–268. https://doi.org/10.1080/14725860903309203.

Chalfen, R. (2010). Commentary sexting as adolescent social communication. *Journal of Children and Media,* 4(3), 350–354. https://doi.org/10.1080/17482798.2010.486144.

Choi, H., Van Ouytsel, J., & Temple, J. R. (2016). Association between sexting and sexual coercion among female adolescents. *Journal of Adolescence, 53,* 164–168. https://doi.org/10.1016/j.adolescence.2016.10.005.

Curnutt, H. (2012). Flashing your phone: Sexting and the remediation of teen sexuality. *Communication Quarterly, 60*(3), 353–369. https://doi.org/10.1080/01463373.2012.688728.

Dir, A. L., Cyders, M. A., & Coskunpinar, A. (2013). From the bar to the bed via mobile phone: A first test of the role of problematic alcohol use, sexting, and impulsivity-related traits in sexual hookups. *Computers in Human Behavior, 29*(4), 1664–1670. https://doi.org/10.1016/j.chb.2013.01.039.

Draper, N. R. A. (2011). Is your teen at risk? Discourses of adolescent sexting in United States television news. *Journal of Children and Media, 6*(2), 221–236. https://doi.org/10.1080/17482798.2011.587147.

Drouin, M., Coupe, M., & Temple, J. R. (2017). Is sexting good for your relationship? It depends .... *Computers in Human Behavior, 75,* 749–756. https://doi.org/10.1016/j.chb.2017.06.018.

Drouin, M., Ross, J., & Tobin, E. (2015). Sexting: A new, digital vehicle for intimate partner aggression? *Computers in Human Behavior, 50*(0), 197–204. https://doi.org/10.1016/j.chb.2015.04.001.

Drouin, M., Vogel, K. N., Surbey, A., & Stills, J. R. (2013). Let's talk about sexting, baby: Computer-mediated sexual behaviors among young adults. *Computers in Human Behavior, 29.* https://doi.org/10.1016/j.chb.2012.12.030.

Edgley, C., & Kiser, K. (1982). Polaroid sex: Deviant possibilities in a technological age. *Journal of American Culture, 5*(1), 59–64.

Englander, E. K. (2015). Coerced sexting and revenge porn among teens. *Bullying, Teen Aggression & Social Media, 1,* 19–21.

Houck, C. D., Barker, D., Rizzo, C., Hancock, E., Norton, A., & Brown, L. K. (2014). Sexting and sexual behavior in at-risk adolescents. *Pediatrics, 133*(2), e276–e282. https://doi.org/10.1542/peds.2013-1157.

Le, V. D., Temple, J. R., Peskin, M., Markham, C., & Tortolero, S. (2014). Sexual behavior and communication. In T. C. Hiestand & W. J. Weins (Eds.), *Sexting and youth; A multidisciplinary examination of research, theory, and law* (pp. 63–94). Durham, NC: Carolina Academic Press.

Lee, C.-H., Moak, S., & Walker, J. T. (2016). Effects of self-control, social control, and social learning on sexting behavior among South Korean youths.

Youth & Society, 48(2), 242–264. https://doi.org/10.1177/00441 18x13490762.

Lenhart, A. (2009). *Teens and sexting*. Washington, DC: Pew Research Center.

Lippman, J. R., & Campbell, S. W. (2014). Damned if you do, damned if you don't…if you're a girl: Relational and normative contexts of adolescent sexting in the United States. *Journal of Children and Media, 8*(4), 371–386. https://doi.org/10.1080/17482798.2014.923009.

Livingstone, S., & Görzig, A. (2012). Sexting: The exchange of sexual messages online among European youth. In S. Livingstone, L. Haddon, & A. Görzig (Eds.), *Children, risk and safety online: Research and policy challenges in comparative perspective* (pp. 149–162). Bristol, UK: The Policy Press.

McDaniel, B. T., & Drouin, M. (2015). Sexting among married couples: Who is doing it, and are they more satisfied? *Cyberpsychology, Behavior, and Social Networking, 18*(11), 628–634. https://doi.org/10.1089/cyber.2015.0334.

Parker, T. S., Blackburn, K. M., Perry, M. S., & Hawks, J. M. (2012). Sexting as an intervention: Relationship satisfaction and motivation considerations. *The American Journal of Family Therapy, 41*(1), 1–12. https://doi.org/10.1080/01926187.2011.635134.

Perkins, A. B., Becker, J. V., Tehee, M., & Mackelprang, E. (2013). Sexting behaviors among college students: Cause for concern? *International Journal of Sexual Health, 26*(2), 79–92. https://doi.org/10.1080/19317611.2013.841 792.

Rice, E., Gibbs, J., Winetrobe, H., Rhoades, H., Plant, A., Montoya, J., & Kordic, T. (2014). Sexting and sexual behavior among middle school students. *Pediatrics*. https://doi.org/10.1542/peds.2013-2991.

Rice, E., Rhoades, H., Winetrobe, H., Sanchez, M., Montoya, J., Plant, A., & Kordic, T. (2012). Sexually explicit cell phone messaging associated with sexual risk among adolescents. *Pediatrics, 130*(4), 667–673. https://doi.org/10.1542/peds.2012-0021.

Ricketts, M., Maloney, C., Marcum, C., & Higgins, G. (2015). The effect of internet related problems on the sexting behaviors of juveniles. *American Journal of Criminal Justice, 40*(2), 270–284. https://doi.org/10.1007/s12103-014-9247-5.

Ringrose, J., Harvey, L., Gill, R., & Livingstone, S. (2013). Teen girls, sexual double standards and 'sexting': Gendered value in digital image exchange. *Feminist Theory, 14*(3), 305–323. https://doi.org/10.1177/1464700113499853.

Romito, P., & Beltramini, L. (2015). Factors associated with exposure to violent or degrading pornography among high school students. *The Journal of School Nursing, 31*(4), 280–290. https://doi.org/10.1177/1059840514563313.

Stanley, N., Barter, C., Wood, M., Aghtaie, N., Larkins, C., Lanau, A., & Överlien, C. (2016). Pornography, sexual coercion and abuse and sexting in young people's intimate relationships: A European study. *Journal of Interpersonal Violence*, 1–26. https://doi.org/10.1177/0886260516633204.

Steinberg, L. (2011). *Adolescence. 9th international edition*. New York: McGraw-Hill Humanities.

Strohmaier, H., Murphy, M., & DeMatteo, D. (2014). Youth sexting: Prevalence rates, driving motivations, and the deterrent effect of legal consequences. *Sexuality Research and Social Policy*, *11*(3), 245–255. https://doi.org/10.1007/s13178-014-0162-9.

Temple, J. R., & Choi, H. (2014). Longitudinal association between teen sexting and sexual behavior. *Pediatrics*, *134*(5), e1287–e1292. https://doi.org/10.1542/peds.2014-1974.

Temple, J. R., Paul, J. A., van den Berg, P., Le, V. D., McElhany, A., & Temple, B. W. (2012). Teen sexting and its association with sexual behaviors. *Archives of Pediatrics & Adolescent Medicine*, *166*(9), 828–833. https://doi.org/10.1001/archpediatrics.2012.835.

van Oosten, J. M. F., & Vandenbosch, L. (2017). Sexy online self-presentation on social network sites and the willingness to engage in sexting: A comparison of gender and age. *Journal of Adolescence*, *54*, 42–50. https://doi.org/10.1016/j.adolescence.2016.11.006.

Van Ouytsel, J., Ponnet, K., & Walrave, M. (2014). The associations between adolescents' consumption of pornography and music videos and their sexting behavior. *Cyberpsychology, Behavior, and Social Networking*, *17*(12), 772–778. https://doi.org/10.1089/cyber.2014.0365.

Van Ouytsel, J., Ponnet, K., Walrave, M., & d'Haenens, L. (2017). Adolescent sexting from a social learning perspective. *Telematics and Informatics*, *34*(1), 287–298. https://doi.org/10.1016/j.tele.2016.05.009.

Van Ouytsel, J., Walrave, M., Ponnet, K., & Heirman, W. (2015). The association between adolescent sexting, psychosocial difficulties, and risk behavior: Integrative review. *The Journal of School Nursing*, *31*(1), 54–69. https://doi.org/10.1177/1059840514541964.

Walker, S., Sanci, L., & Temple-Smith, M. (2013). Sexting: Young women's and men's views on its nature and origins. *Journal of Adolescent Health*, *52*(6), 697–701. https://doi.org/10.1016/j.jadohealth.2013.01.026.

Walrave, M., Heirman, W., & Hallam, L. (2014). Under pressure to sext? Applying the theory of planned behaviour to adolescent sexting. *Behaviour & Information Technology*, *33*(1), 86–98. https://doi.org/10.1080/0144929X.2013.837099.

Walrave, M., Ponnet, K., Van Ouytsel, J., Van Gool, E., Heirman, W., & Verbeek, A. (2015). Whether or not to engage in sexting: Explaining adolescent sexting behaviour by applying the prototype willingness model. *Telematics and Informatics*, *32*(4), 796–808. https://doi.org/10.1016/j.tele.2015.03.008.

Wysocki, D. K., & Childers, C. D. (2011). "Let my fingers do the talking": Sexting and infidelity in cyberspace. *Sexuality & Culture, 15*(3), 217–239. https://doi.org/10.1007/s12119-011-9091-4.

Ybarra, M. L., & Mitchell, K. J. (2014). "Sexting" and its relation to sexual activity and sexual risk behavior in a National survey of adolescents. *Journal of Adolescent Health, 55*(6), 757–764. https://doi.org/10.1016/j.jadohealth.2014.07.012.

CHAPTER 4

Sexting from a Health Perspective: Sexting, Health, and Risky Sexual Behaviour

Jeff R. Temple and Yu Lu

Abstract With the advent and ubiquity of smartphones being less than a decade old, it is not surprising that research on teen sexting is in its infancy. Although it has consistently been shown that sexting is related to actual sexual behaviour, research on the link between sexting and adverse health outcomes is less clear. The current chapter will review the evidence examining the link between teen sexting and (1) sexual behaviour, (2) risky sexual behaviour, and (3) psychosocial health. Practical strategies will be provided on how to address sexting with teens and teens' parents, when concerns about sexting are justified, and potential methods to prevent coercive sexting. Arguments will be supported with original data from an ongoing longitudinal study of adolescent health.

Keywords Sexting • Sexual behaviour • Risky sexual behaviour • Psychosocial health

J. R. Temple (✉) • Y. Lu
Department of Obstetrics & Gynecology, Behavioral Health and Research, UTMB, Galveston, TX, USA

© The Author(s) 2018
M. Walrave et al. (eds.), *Sexting*, Palgrave Studies in Cyberpsychology,
https://doi.org/10.1007/978-3-319-71882-8_4

Introduction

Research on teen sexting (herein defined as the sharing of sexually explicit messages, images, or videos through electronic means) has increased substantially over the past several years. We are beginning to grasp the prevalence of sexting among teens in general, as well as differences by age, gender, and ethnicity. We know that sexting is related to offline sexual behaviour (Klettke, Hallford, & Mellor, 2014), and may even be a marker for future sexual activity (Temple & Choi, 2014). Less known, however, is whether and how sexting is related to risky behaviours and psychological health. This lack of clear findings makes it difficult for schools, communities, and health care providers to address this emerging phenomenon. The current chapter will review the evidence examining the link between teen sexting and (1) sexual behaviour, (2) risky sexual behaviour, and (3) psychosocial health. Practical strategies will be provided on how to address sexting with teens and teens' parents, on how to know when concerns about sexting are justified, and potential methods to prevent coercive sexting.

Sexting and Sexual Behaviour

Given the prevalence of teens sending sexts, its link to sexual activity has been a point of emphasis. Unsurprisingly, studies consistently reveal a robust link between sexting and real life sexual behaviour. In fact, in a recent review of the literature of 31 articles about sexting prevalence and related variables, Klettke et al. (2014) concluded that all eight papers (at that time) examining this link between sexting and sexual activities detected an association. That is, those who had reported previously sexting were significantly more likely to be sexually active than non-sexters. In our study (Temple et al., 2012) of 948 adolescents in 10th or 11th grades in Texas we found that 82% of boys who had sent a sext had had sex, whereas only 45% of non-sexting boys had had sex. Similarly, 77% of girls who had sent a sext had had sex versus 42% of girls who had not sexted. In another study, Rice and colleagues (Rice et al., 2017) examined sexual behaviour and its associations with different forms of sexting (i.e., not sending or receiving sexts, sexting, only receiving sexts, both sending and receiving sexts) among 1208 mobile phone-owning teens in Los Angles. It was found that compared to not sending or receiving sexts, receiving sexts and both sending and receiving sexts were associated with lifetime sexual intercourse, anal sex, and oral sex experiences. Overall, based on a recent meta-analysis (Kosenko, Luurs, & Binder, 2017), sexting is associated with sexual behaviours with a moderate effective size of .35.

While sexting may be a gateway to actual sexual behaviours, possibly by inviting sexual advances or as a way to indicate willingness to engage in sex, it could be that having sex increases comfort level and flirtation, potentially resulting in sexting behaviour. Determining the temporal relationship between sexting and sexual activity has important implications for prevention and intervention programs. Indeed, if sexting precedes sexual behaviour, we can educate sexting teens on the importance of healthy relationships and safe sexual behaviour. In one of the only longitudinal studies to date (Temple & Choi, 2014), we found that the odds of being sexually active one year later were 1.32 times larger for high school youth who sent a sext, relative to their non-sexting teen counterparts. Similarly, in a study by Brinkley and colleagues (Brinkley, Ackerman, Ehrenreich, & Underwood, 2017), sexting at age 16 was linked to having sexual experiences two years later. Existing evidence supports the notion that sexting may be a gateway to sexual behaviour and highlights the importance of sexual education for teens who engage in sexting. It also implies the possibility of delaying teen sexual introduction by preventing sexting at a young age. Overall, the link between sexting and sexual behaviour is well established and has important implications for teen healthy relationships.

Sexting and Risky Sexual Behaviour

The link between sexting and risky sexual behaviour is less clear, with some studies showing a relation and others finding no association. For example, in our study (Temple et al., 2012) we found that adolescent girls who sexted, relative to non-sexting girls, were more likely to partake in risky sexual behaviours, including having multiple sexual partners and using drugs and alcohol prior to last sexual activity. However, when looked at longitudinally, the link between sexting and risky sexual behaviour did not emerge. Similarly, while Ferguson (2011) found a link between sexting and lack of birth control use in a sample of Hispanic young women aged 16–25, no other associations were found. In a study of 1285 middle school students in Los Angeles, among sexually active youth, sexting adolescents (sent and received) were substantially more likely to have engaged in unprotected sex.

However, sexting youth were also more likely to have protected sex (Rice et al., 2014). Because this sample was composed of young adolescents, any sexual activity could be interpreted as risky (indeed, early sexual debut is related to numerous negative psychosocial consequences) (Sandfort, Orr, Hirsch, & Santelli, 2008). Thus, that youth who received and sent sexts were six and four times more likely, respectively, than their non-sexting counterparts to be sexually active is noteworthy. The authors argue that sexting education should become part of middle-school curricula, as well as extend to the home and paediatrician.

Brinkley and colleagues (2017) found that sexting was longitudinally related to early sexual debut, larger number of sex partners, and using drugs at the time of sexual activity. Similarly, in a group of 1372 Australians aged 16–29 (Yeung, Horyniak, Vella, Hellard, & Lim, 2014), sexting was associated with greater lifetime number of sexual partners and inconsistent condom use with a regular partner. Rice and colleagues (2017) also found that teens who receive sexts and those who both send and receive sexts are more likely than their non-sexting peers to report unprotected sex. A recent meta-analysis (Kosenko et al., 2017) concluded that sexting was positively associated with both unprotected sex and number of sex partners, although both effect sizes were small (i.e., $\leq .20$). Given the weak associations, Kosenko and colleagues argued that sexting may not be a particular good indicator of risky sexual behaviours and suggested future research focusing on how sexting links to other problem behaviours.

Overall, studies about sexting and risky sexual behaviours show mixed findings. Given that the majority of sexting studies to date utilize cross-sectional data, it is important to note that no research exists suggesting that sexting causes, or even directly contributes to, sex or risky sex. It is possible that these behaviours are the opposite side of the same coin; that an underlying variable (pubertal timing, sexual identity development, participating in risky behaviours) is independently linked to online sexual and offline sexual behaviours.

SEXTING AND PSYCHOSOCIAL HEALTH

The link between sexting and psychosocial health is inconsistent, at best. While we found an association between sexting and a host of mental health and risky behaviours, these significant findings mostly vanished when we controlled for prior sexual behaviour (Temple et al., 2014). Indeed, in the adjusted models, only impulsivity and substance use were significantly related to sexting. This is similar to a study by Gordon-Messer and colleagues (Gordon-Messer, Bauermeister, Grodzinski, & Zimmerman, 2013), in which self-esteem, depression, and anxiety were not related to sexting. Relatedly, O'Sullivan (2014) did not find a link between sexting and several psychological health variables. A study of Italian adolescents revealed no differences with respect to psychological distress among three groups of sexters (i.e., non-sexters, moderate sexters, and high sexters). The limited research on emerging adults has demonstrated a link between sexting and substance use (Benotsch, Snipes, Martin, & Bull, 2013), but not between sexting and psychological health (Gordon-Messer et al., 2013). For example, Benotsch and colleagues linked sexting to use of alcohol, marijuana, ecstasy, and cocaine. Yeung and colleagues (Yeung et al., 2014) also found in a sample of Australian young people aged 16–29 that sexting was associated with excessive alcohol consumption resulting in either injury to self or others or regular memory loss. In addition to substance use, and converse to the above findings, others have found an association between sexting and psychological distress (Dake, Price, Maziarz, & Ward, 2012). For instance, Brinkley and colleagues (Brinkley et al., 2017) found that sexting (specifically, hypothetical sex talk) was longitudinally linked to borderline features. Similarly, Van Ouytsel and colleagues (Van Ouytsel, Van Gool, Ponnet, & Walrave, 2014) found that teens who sexted were more likely than these who did not to report depressive symptoms.

The equivocal findings with respect to sexting and psychological health may be due to the fact that most studies do not distinguish between wanted and unwanted or coerced sexts. As with adolescent (offline) sexual behaviour, it is likely that sexting between willing intimate partners is developmentally common and not expected to be associated with poor psychological health. When coerced, on the other hand, it can be expected to be linked to feelings of guilt, shame, and embarrassment. This is especially true considering our recent finding that sexting is related to sexual coercion offline (Choi, Van Ouytsel, & Temple, 2016). Indeed, a qualitative study conducted in Belgium reported that girls may feel pressured in engaging in sexting in fear of losing their boyfriend (Van Ouytsel, Van Gool, Walrave, Ponnet, & Peeters, 2017). Furthermore, the transient nature of teen relationships may increase the likelihood of sexted images being disseminated beyond the intended audience (e.g., romantic partner), potentially resulting in subsequent psychological distress (Lenhart,

2009), or in rare and extreme cases, suicide, due to bullying and harassment resulted from sexting (O'Sullivan, 2014). Future research should distinguish between the contexts of sexting, especially willingly versus coerced, to further examine the link between sexting and psychosocial health.

SEXTING EDUCATION

Given the prevalence of sexting, tweens and teens should be provided education on digital citizenship, and be informed of potential consequences. First, youth should know about the possibilities of their sexts being disseminated to people other than the targeted audience and the potential consequences thereof (Rice et al., 2014). This could be general education on internet privacy or specific sessions about sexting. More importantly, youth should learn general healthy relationship skills, which will help them positively interact with others and make better decisions when it comes to risky behaviours, including sexting (especially with respect to not use sexting as a vehicle to abuse or bully others). This can be achieved by implementing school-based anti-bullying, violence prevention, and healthy relationship programs. For example, a comprehensive school-based program, *Fourth R*, targets shared risk and protective factors of multiple risk behaviours and has been shown to improve healthy relationship skills in youth (Wolfe et al., 2009). Other individual approaches include providing information through out-of-school platforms such as text message based campaigns, video game intervention that enables youth to practice prosocial skills, to name a few (Peskin et al., 2014). As shown in our own school-based healthy relationship campaign, adolescents have reported cases when they decided to delete a sext received from friends (instead of sharing it with others).

For parents and caregivers, it is important to be aware that sexting is becoming common among teens in this digital age. We should respect teens' autonomy and intelligence, and refrain from using scare tactics, especially given that there is not enough evidence supporting a causal link between sexting and adverse outcomes, such as risky sexual behaviour and psychological distress. Sexting may be a gateway to sexual behaviours or could be considered as a new type of sexual behaviour. When teens are found sexting, it can be used as an opportunity for sexual education, such as a discussion on healthy relationships, to prevent early sexual introduction, and promote safe sexual practices. With respect to digital citizenship more generally, parents/caregivers should become more familiar with technology and treat the online world just as they would any other environment; that is, set limits, know who their children are talking to and who they are friends with, and know what apps and websites they are visiting (American Association of Pediatrics, 2015). See below for specific recommendations regarding teen sexting (modified from Temple, 2015).

For All Parents, Caregivers, and Healthcare Providers of Tweens and Teens
- "the talk" is an ongoing conversation that should start early and emphasize healthy relationships and positive sexual education.
- Familiarize yourself and stay current with advances in technology.
- Download and learn popular sharing apps like Instagram and Snapchat. Speaking their "language" lends you credibility.
- For parents of younger kids, "friend", "follow", or "like" their accounts.
- For parents of older kids, where autonomy is critical to development, parents may opt to allow more privacy. Treat their online world as you would their offline world. For example, know who their friends are, what sites they frequent.
- For parents, talk to your kids about sexting. Be sure they know the potential risks associated with sending, storing, and spreading nude pictures.
- For healthcare providers, consider asking your patients – especially younger adolescents – about sexting, as this behaviour may be indicative of sexual activity, and possible risky sexual activity.
- Avoid scare tactics such as: "If you send a nude photo, you'll never get into college or get a good job." While this may happen, it is unlikely, and you may lose any credibility you had on the subject.
- Advocate for schools and the local community to provide comprehensive sexual education and digital citizenship curricula.

Conclusion

The public health importance of sexting may rest on it cross-sectional and longitudinal relationship to sexual behaviour, including potentially risky sexual behaviour. With respect to the former, research consistently and robustly reveals a clear link. The research is less clear on the latter, but the equivocal findings warrant additional research. That the link between sexting and psychological health is mixed may suggest the presence of an underlying third variable such as being coerced to sext. The nature and prevalence of sexting among teens calls for sexting education. Adolescents should be educated about the potential consequences and acquire relationship knowledge and skills to handle it properly. Parents and caregivers should have an open discussion with teens who are sexting and use this as an opportunity for sexual education.

References

American Association of Pediatrics. (2015). *Children and media – Tips for parents.* https://www.aap.org/en-us/about-the-aap/aap-press-room/pages/children-and-media-tips-for-parents.aspx

Benotsch, E. G., Snipes, D. J., Martin, A. M., & Bull, S. S. (2013). Sexting, substance use, and sexual risk behavior in young adults. *Journal of Adolescent Health, 52*(3), 307–313.

Brinkley, D. Y., Ackerman, R. A., Ehrenreich, S. E., & Underwood, M. K. (2017). Sending and receiving text messages with sexual content: Relations with early sexual activity and borderline personality features in late adolescence. *Computers in Human Behavior, 70*, 119–130.

Choi, H., Van Ouytsel, J., & Temple, J. R. (2016). Association between sexting and sexual coercion among female adolescents. *Journal of Adolescence, 53*, 164–168.

Dake, J. A., Price, J. H., Maziarz, L., & Ward, B. (2012). Prevalence and correlates of sexting behavior in adolescents. *American Journal of Sexuality Education, 7*(1), 1–15.

Ferguson, C. J. (2011). Sexting behaviors among young Hispanic women: Incidence and association with other high-risk sexual behaviors. *Psychiatric Quarterly, 82*(3), 239–243.

Gordon-Messer, D., Bauermeister, J. A., Grodzinski, A., & Zimmerman, M. (2013). Sexting among young adults. *Journal of Adolescent Health, 52*(3), 301–306.

Klettke, B., Hallford, D. J., & Mellor, D. J. (2014). Sexting prevalence and correlates: A systematic literature review. *Clinical Psychology Review, 34*(1), 44–53.

Kosenko, K., Luurs, G., & Binder, A. R. (2017). Sexting and sexual behavior, 2011–2015: A critical review and meta – Analysis of a growing literature. *Journal of Computer – Mediated Communication, 22*(3), 141–160.

Lenhart, A. (2009). *Teens and sexting.* http://ncdsv.org/images/PewInternet_TeensAndSexting_12-2009.pdf

O'Sullivan, L. F. (2014). Linking online sexual activities to health outcomes among teens. *New Directions for Child and Adolescent Development, 2014*(144), 37–51.

Peskin, M. F., Markham, C. M., Shegog, R., Baumler, E. R., Addy, R. C., et al. (2014). Effects of the It's your game... keep it real program on dating violence in ethnic-minority middle school youths: A group randomized trial. *American Journal of Public Health, 104*(8), 1471–1477.

Rice, E., Craddock, J., Hemler, M., Rusow, J., Plant, A., Montoya, J., et al. (2017). Associations between sexting behaviors and sexual behaviors among mobile phone-owning teens in Los Angeles. *Child Development.* Advance online publication.

Rice, E., Gibbs, J., Winetrobe, H., Rhoades, H., Plant, A., Montoya, J., et al. (2014). Sexting and sexual behavior among middle school students. *Pediatrics, 134*(1), e21–e28.

Sandfort, T. G., Orr, M., Hirsch, J. S., & Santelli, J. (2008). Long-term health correlates of timing of sexual debut: Results from a national US study. *American Journal of Public Health, 98*(1), 155–161.

Temple, J. R. (2015). A primer on teen sexting. *Journal of the American Academy of Child and Adolescent Psychiatry Connect, 2,* 6–8.

Temple, J. R., & Choi, H. (2014). Longitudinal association between teen sexting and sexual behavior. *Pediatrics, 134*(5), e1287–e1292.

Temple, J. R., Le, V. D., van den Berg, P., Ling, Y., Paul, J. A., & Temple, B. W. (2014). Brief report: Teen sexting and psychosocial health. *Journal of Adolescence, 37*(1), 33–36.

Temple, J. R., Paul, J. A., van den Berg, P., Le, V. D., McElhany, A., & Temple, B. W. (2012). Teen sexting and its association with sexual behaviors. *Archives of Pediatrics and Adolescent Medicine, 166*(9), 828–833.

Van Ouytsel, J., Van Gool, E., Ponnet, K., & Walrave, M. (2014). Brief report: The association between adolescents' characteristics and engagement in sexting. *Journal of Adolescence, 37*(8), 1387–1391.

Van Ouytsel, J., Van Gool, E., Walrave, M., Ponnet, K., & Peeters, E. (2017). Sexting: Adolescents' perceptions of the applications used for, motives for, and consequences of sexting. *Journal of Youth Studies, 20*(4), 446–470.

Wolfe, A. D., Crooks, C. V., Jaffe, P. G., Chiodo, D., Hughes, R., et al. (2009). A universal school-based program to prevent adolescent dating violence: A cluster randomized trial. *Archives of Pediatric and Adolescent Medicine, 163,* 693–699.

Yeung, T. H., Horyniak, D. R., Vella, A. M., Hellard, M. E., & Lim, M. S. (2014). Prevalence, correlates and attitudes towards sexting among young people in Melbourne, Australia. *Sexual Health, 11*(4), 332–339.

CHAPTER 5

Parents' Role in Adolescents' Sexting Behaviour

Ini Vanwesenbeeck, Koen Ponnet, Michel Walrave,
and Joris Van Ouytsel

Abstract In this chapter we provide an overview of parental styles that are used by parents, the application of these parental styles towards media use and the parental mediation of sexual behaviour of adolescents. In adolescents' relational and sexual development, parents may play a role in addressing health risks. As sexting has become a part of intimate communication for adolescents, sexting related risks could be addressed in parents' sex education. Therefore, we integrate the findings of several studies on parenting and discuss which implications parenting may have for

I. Vanwesenbeeck (✉)
Department of Communication Sciences, CEPEC, Ghent University,
Ghent, Belgium

K. Ponnet
Department of Communication Studies, MIOS, University of Antwerp,
Antwerp, Belgium

Department of Communication Sciences, IMEC-MICT, Ghent University,
Ghent, Belgium

M. Walrave • J. Van Ouytsel
Department of Communication Studies, MIOS, University of Antwerp,
Antwerp, Belgium

© The Author(s) 2018   63
M. Walrave et al. (eds.), *Sexting*, Palgrave Studies in Cyberpsychology,
https://doi.org/10.1007/978-3-319-71882-8_5

sexting behaviour. Investigating how parenting and parental styles could impact upon sexting behaviour is important, as this could lead to practical recommendations to parents on how to prevent and deal with sexting related risks.

Keywords Sexting • Parenting • Sex education • Parenting styles • Parental internet mediation

INTRODUCTION

Contemporary adolescents spend a significant part of their lives in the online world. Being online is a popular activity among teenagers, because it offers them a platform for self-presentation and self-disclosure. However, given that adolescence is often characterized by experimentation and risk taking, adolescents might also engage in online risk behaviours, like sexting (Draper, 2012; Lau & Yuen, 2013). Sexting is defined as "electronically sending sexually explicit images from one adolescent to another" (Temple et al., 2014, p. 33) and is often referred to as an example of risk behaviour, as sexting poses potential harm to adolescents (Johnston, 2016). This behaviour can happen at all ages, but research has confirmed that sexting is more prevalent during adolescence (Johnston, 2016). Research has already established that several factors can impact upon adolescents' sexting behaviour. Most importantly, peer influence plays a key role in sexting behaviour (Walrave et al., 2015). Sexting can be a common practice among adolescents as the behaviour can be a way to explore their sexuality (Baumgartner, Sumter, Peter, & Valkenburg, 2012; Campbell & Park, 2014). Still, sexting can lead to a number of negative consequences. In a few clicks, a sender of a sexting message can potentially lose control over his/hers sexual explicit photo (Draper, 2012). Furthermore, sexting can occur under pressure or within the context of an abusive romantic relationship (Choi, Van Ouytsel, & Temple, 2016; Van Ouytsel, Ponnet, & Walrave, 2016). Therefore, it is important to investigate how adolescents can be empowered to deal with sexting and its associated risks.

Adolescence is characterized by a transition from child-to-adulthood, with increased levels of autonomy and the development of identity (Baumrind, 1991; Valkenburg, Piotrowski, Hermanns, & Leeuw, 2013). During adolescence, social relationships outside the family environment become increasingly important (Sasson & Mesch, 2014). Given adolescents'

susceptibility to their peers' opinions, researchers often suggest that adolescents are less influenced by their parents (Campbell & Park, 2014; Valkenburg et al., 2013). Within the relationship with their parents, adolescents often test the boundaries of rules and limits (Valkenburg et al., 2013). Consequently, adolescents are not always inclined to comply with their family standards (Valkenburg et al., 2013). Still, parents often remain the primary socialization agents during adolescence (Otten, Engels, van de Ven, & Bricker, 2007). Therefore, during adolescence, parents should be even more aware of choosing the right parental mediation style. If handled the wrong way, adolescents may even be prone to reactance effects, which can lead to the exact opposite behaviour of what is expected from them (Valkenburg et al., 2013). One major problem that parents experience is that they find it difficult to balance between on the one hand respecting their teen's privacy and giving them autonomy and on the other hand preventing them from harm risks (Yardi & Bruckman, 2011).

This chapter contributes to the current knowledge of how parents mediate to their children's online behaviour, and sexting in particular. We provide evidence that parents can play a significant role in educating their children about the risks and consequences of sexting. To the best of our knowledge, only a handful of studies have touched upon the topic on parental styles and sexting (Baumgartner et al., 2012; Haddon, Loos, Haddon, & Mante-Meijer, 2012; Houck et al., 2014). As parents are important actors in adolescents' lives, it is relevant to describe how parents can assist their offspring in dealing with sexting behaviour. Therefore, we first provide an overview of parental styles that are used by parents. Then, we describe the application of these parental styles towards media use and the parental mediation of relational and sexual behaviour of adolescents. Thereafter, we integrate the above-mentioned insights and discuss what implication parental mediation may have for sexting behaviour. Investigating how parenting and parental strategies could impact upon sexting behaviour is important, as this could lead to practical recommendations to parents on how to prevent and deal with sexting behaviour.

PARENTING STYLES

Almost three decades ago, Baumrind (1991) defined parenting as the general emotional climate in which child rearing takes place, an idea also endorsed by Darling and Steinberg (1993). Parenting, according to Baumrind (1991), varies according to two independent dimensions:

parental warmth and parental control. Parental warmth, often described as parental responsiveness, refers to the investment and support parents give to their children (Lau & Yuen, 2013; Valcke, Bonte, De Wever, & Rots, 2010). Parental control, also referred to as parental demandingness, encompasses the amount of rules and control parents exert on their children (Valcke et al., 2010). Parental control can be exercised in two ways, behavioural parental control and psychological parental control. Psychological control refers to parental control that impacts upon children's psychological and emotional development, while behavioural control refers to managing children's behaviour (Barber, 1996). Especially psychological control has been discussed in literature as a negative way to exercise control (Barber, 1996).

Although parenting styles and parenting practices are often treated interchangeably, they are two distinct variables. Parenting practices are directed toward particular goals, while parenting styles can be regarded as the general context or climate within which the more specific parenting practices are expressed (Darling & Steinberg, 1993). In other words, parenting styles prevail across different socialization contents and contexts. Relying on the two abovementioned dimensions warmth and control, Baumrind (1991) distinguished four key parenting styles: authoritative, authoritarian, permissive, and uninvolved. Authoritative parents combine high levels of support and control. This is considered the most effective parenting style for promoting children's well-being. Authoritarian parents provide high control and low support, and as such are often seen as restrictive when interacting with their children (Walsh, Laczniak, & Carlson, 1998). Permissive parents provide high support and low control. Finally, uninvolved parents provide low support and low control (Bastaits, Pasteels, Ponnet, & Mortelmans, 2015). Uninvolved parents are detached from their children and do not provide their children with parental warmth (Eastin, Greenberg, & Hofschire, 2006). As a consequence, children from parents using such a parenting style may even count more on other socialization agents, such as their peers (Walsh et al., 1998). In general, the authoritative parenting style leads to the most positive consequences. Still, for some children, an authoritarian or permissive parenting style might also be effective. No evidence however have been found that the neglecting parenting style leads to better outcomes for children and adolescents (Eastin et al., 2006).

Several studies have demonstrated that mothers spend significantly more time with their (young) children than fathers do. As a result, early research on parenting styles tended to focus solely on mothers' being

responsible for the adjustment of their children and adolescents (Phares, Fields, & Kamboukos, 2009). The past decade, research has started to focus on the importance of fathers (e.g., their behaviours, parenting styles) for the outcome of their children. A more contemporary theory, the role theory, states that the mother role has been traditionally defined as that of caregiver; thus, women become socialized to provide warmth and care for their children (McKinney & Renk, 2008). In contrast, the father role has been traditionally defined as that of a provider and being authoritarian. As a result, men become socialized to assume these roles to the exclusion of providing warmth and care for their children. Support for this comes from the findings that fathers have traditionally experienced little involvement in and responsibility for providing care for their children. Still, the past two decades, fathers seem more involved in rearing their children than some time ago. Although most fathers do not take as active a role in the parenting process as most mothers, the gap between men's and women's participation in childrearing appears to be shrinking (Amato, Meyers, & Emery, 2009; Lamb, 2010; Woodworth, Belsky, & Crnic, 1996).

Role theory may also account for differences in the parenting of sons and daughters. For instance, there is some evidence that parents use more sensitive or autonomy-supportive strategies with girls than with boys and more harsh or controlling strategies with boys than with girls (Kochanska, Barry, Stellern, & O'Bleness, 2009; Mandara, Murray, Telesford, Varner, & Richman, 2012; Tamis-LeMonda, Briggs, McClowry, & Snow, 2009). These findings indicate that parents may prefer to use more controlling strategies (i.e., focused on dominance, negativity, and power) with boys, and autonomy-supportive strategies (i.e., focused on warmth, affiliation, and interpersonal closeness) more with girls. However, there is also a number of studies that does not find evidence that parents use control differently with boys and girls (Endendijk, Groeneveld, Bakermans-Kranenburg, & Mesman, 2016), and some studies even provide evidence that parents use more autonomy-supportive strategies with boys than with girls, and are more controlling of girls than of boys (Domenech Rodriguez, Donovick, & Crowley, 2009).

Parental Mediation Theory

Parental mediation theory is closely related the abovementioned parental styles, and refers to how parents regulate children's and adolescent's media use (Eastin et al., 2006). Parental mediation strategies have been found to influence children's media use (Rosen, Cheever, & Carrier, 2008; Shin, Huh, & Faber, 2012; Valcke et al., 2010). The call for increased parental mediation initially arose from a concern of children's exposure to violent and sexual TV content (Warren, 2001). Therefore, although the first parental mediation theories focussed on TV advertising, the parental mediation theory can be applied to media in general (Livingstone & Helsper, 2007).

Based on parents' reports on their engagement in a range of thirty mediation practices, with reference to the television viewing of a child aged five to twelve, Valkenburg et al. (1999) achieved a classification of three parental mediation styles. First, restrictive mediation relates to parents' strategies to control media access and restrict the time that their children spend with media (Livingstone, 2007; Valkenburg et al., 2013). Second, active mediation refers to parents' attempt to actively explain media content to their children and convey their opinion (Valkenburg et al., 2013). In other words, parents using active mediation explain and discuss (undesirable) aspects of media content. The third parental mediation style is coviewing, which refers to parents viewing media content together with their children (Nathanson, 2001). Coviewing does not entail that parents discuss media content with their children (Eastin et al., 2006). Further, the interpretation of coviewing is different for digital media compared to television. While TV viewing is a social activity within the family, children have the tendency to isolate themselves while using the internet. For adolescents, the internet is considered as a private space (Borca, Bina, Keller, Gilbert, & Begotti, 2015). This is also reflected in the devices that are used by families. For instance, families often consider the tablet as a personal device, instead of a shared one (Vanhaelewyn & De Marez, 2016). Coviewing is less studied in the context of new media. However, it is interesting to note that when children do watch online content together with their parents, this is likely to be more accompanied by parental advice and guidance, compared to TV viewing (Livingstone & Helpser, 2007). The parental mediation style that parents use impacts upon media effects. Most empirical research established that active mediation is more effective than restrictive mediation in reducing undesirable effects of media (see for example Buijzen et al., 2008; Lwin, Stanaland, & Miyazaki, 2008). For instance, Lwin et al. (2008) established that children whose parents used more active mediation strategies were less likely to disclose sensitive information (such as full name, address and phone number) online. Age and gender are important to take into account with regard to parental mediation styles. Younger adolescents often get more rules and regulations from their parents compared to older adolescents (Livingstone & Helsper, 2007).

Specifically, for online communication, a parental mediation style that is often mentioned in the literature is parental monitoring. Parental monitoring refers to the knowledge that parents have about their children's activities (Stattin & Kerr, 2000) and consists of three aspects: solicitation, control and adolescents' willingness to disclose information to their parents. Solicitation and control both refer to actions that parents undertake to find out what their child is doing (Sasson & Mesch, 2014; Stattin & Kerr, 2000). Given the importance of the internet as a social space for adolescents, parents knowledge also refers to following adolescents' online activities (Sasson & Mesch, 2014), for example by looking into the pages that were visited or by reading personal messages. The third aspect of parental monitoring refers to the adolescent's willingness to disclose information to his/her parents (Stattin & Kerr, 2000). Parental knowledge of adolescents' online experiences may possibly lead to adolescents using the internet more safely. The level of parental knowledge of adolescents' online experiences was investigated by Symons, Ponnet, Emmery, Walrave, and Heirman (2017). In total, 357 families participated (child, mother and father) with the children aged 13 to 18. Parental knowledge of adolescents' online experiences appeared rather low (Symons et al., 2017). Furthermore, the perceived openness of communication in the child's point of view lead to a higher self-perceived knowledge in the mother: the mother reported a higher knowledge with regard to the information the child disclosed online. For fathers, the perceived openness of communication did not have an effect on parental knowledge (Symons et al., 2017).

As children and adolescents' media use has evolved, parental mediation theory has also undergone changes and as a result the classic division between active and restrictive mediation styles has been questioned. Valkenburg et al. (2013) suggested that both restrictive and active mediation can be effective, given that the mediation takes place in a certain way. The perceived parental mediation framework focusses on media in general, instead of solely on television advertising (Valkenburg et al., 2013). Perceived parental media mediation styles reflect how children perceive their parents' media mediation and is based on existing parenting theories (Valkenburg et al., 2013), the most influential of which is the abovementioned Baumrind's classification of parenting styles. Furthermore, the perceived parental media mediation styles draw on self-determination theory (SDT) (Soenens, Vansteenkiste, & Niemiec, 2009) which states that children acquire and accept the rules of a society through social influences. The family has therefore an important influence on the child (Guay, Ratelle, & Chanal, 2008). Accordingly, internalization of values is more likely to happen when children and young adolescents are motivated to comply with the wishes of their parents; this internalization should then lead to the behaviours desired by the parents (Soenens et al., 2009). Children and young adolescents are not always motivated to comply with their parents' wishes, however. The SDT is especially relevant for adolescents, as this theory strongly emphasises the importance of autonomy (Valkenburg et al., 2013). In controlling contexts, under pressure to think or act in specific ways, individuals can no longer act on the basis of their own motivation (Deci & Ryan, 2000). Such situations do not support internalization, as the individuals concerned are not intrinsically motivated to comply with the rules being imposed (Deci & Ryan, 2000). Applied to a media mediation context, Valkenburg et al. (2013) describe three parenting styles: autonomy-supportive parenting, controlling parenting and inconsistent parenting.

Autonomy-Supportive Parenting Following the self-determination theory, autonomy-supportive parenting takes the child's feelings and perspective into account. Valkenburg et al. (2013) translates the autonomy-supportive parenting to a more media-specific parenting. Autonomy-supportive media mediation is defined as parents' restriction or active discussion about media in which a rationale is provided and in which the perspective of the adolescent is taken seriously (Valkenburg et al., 2013, p. 5). An autonomy-supportive contexts is likely to foster internalization, as mediation based on open discussions stimulates critical thinking (Shin et al., 2012). Due to the internalization of rules, an autonomy-supportive media mediation style will more likely result in children following their parents' rules with regard to media usage. In the perceived parental media mediation framework, two styles of autonomy-supportive parental media mediation are distinguished: active and restrictive. Autonomy-supportive active media mediation involves having active discussions of media content, without imposing restrictions and taking the child's point of view into consideration. Autonomy-supportive restrictive parental media mediation involves placing restrictions on media use, albeit with respect for the child's point of view (Valkenburg et al., 2013).

Controlling Parenting Another style of perceived parental media mediation is controlling mediation, in which a child or adolescent is pressured to comply with externally imposed guidelines (Kocayörük et al., 2014; Soenens et al., 2009). For instance, using blocking- and filtering software parents can manage their child's access to certain internet content. In general, controlling parenting styles have been found to have a negative effect on children's and adolescents' development (Soenens & Vansteenkiste, 2010). This style can also take place in a restrictive or active way. Controlling active mediation refers to the parents who actively give their opinion on media content, but without considering the opinions of their children themselves (Valkenburg et al., 2013). Controlling restrictive mediation refers to restricting children's media access by getting angry at the child or threatening their child with punishments (Valkenburg et al., 2013). This type of parental mediation is not assumed to be effective, especially among adolescents, since this can cause reactance effects and wrong internalization of the rules (Valkenburg et al., 2013). The reactance theory (Brehm, 1966) suggests that a person will react against persuasion if they feel that their personal freedom is threatened. A threat to freedom leads to a mental state of arousal, which ultimately leads to a reaction against the desired behaviour (Brehm, 1966; Lwin et al., 2008). Implying rules on media use can cause a child to feel threatened in their freedom (Sneegas & Plank, 1998).

Inconsistent Parenting The perceived parental media mediation framework also describes a third style, namely inconsistent parental media mediation. In terms of restrictive parental media mediation, this style is defined by Valkenburg et al. (2013, p. 6) as "parents' tendency to be erratic and unpredictable in their restriction of time that their children spend with media or the content to which they are exposed". For example, a parent may forbid his/her child to watch a particular program and then allow it a few hours later. This style is also likely to cause reactance effects (Valkenburg et al., 2013).

Parental Styles and Impact on (Sexual) Risk-Taking Behaviour

As mentioned above, developing adolescents have a strong need for autonomy. Mobile communication give them an excellent opportunity to fulfil this need and to let them contact their peers in their own way

(Campbell & Park, 2014). A problem that might arise with parental mediation of online risks, is that children are often more savvy internet users compared to their parents (Draper, 2012; Shin et al., 2012). However, despite being more knowledgeable, their immaturity could lead to risk-taking behaviour and associated negative consequences (Houck et al., 2014). Further, internet use is increasingly becoming a private space for adolescents, leading parents to have limited knowledge on their child's online activities and associated risks (Symons et al., 2017).

Although adolescents often consider their peers as more important than their parents, parents still have a major influence on the risk behaviour of their children (Sasson & Mesch, 2014). Following the parental mediation theory, active mediation, preferably in an autonomy-supportive way, is associated with less risk behaviour. Controlling parenting is associated with a higher level of risk behaviour. Empirical research on risk-behaviour largely supports this. In a study among 495 adolescents, Sasson and Mesch (2014) established that technological control was associated with an higher engagement of adolescents' risky activities. In line with the parenting styles from Baumrind (1991), excessive control does not lead to the desired effects. The risk behaviours investigated in this study were sending an insulting message, posting personal details online and meeting with strangers. Nevertheless, the authors of the study plead for more extensive research on other risky behaviours. Further research on risk behaviour and parental mediation was done by Shin and Ismail (Shin & Ismail, 2014). The study, involving 469 adolescent SNS users (aged 13–14) established that control-based mediation was associated with being more inclined to take risks on social network sites. Further, a higher level of active mediation was associated with reducing contact risks on social network sites (i.e. adding stranger in their own social network), while active mediation did not relate to a reduced privacy concern (Shin & Ismail, 2014). Regarding adolescents' disclosure of personal information to businesses online, research among 12 to 18-year-olds found that both active co-surfing and restrictive mediation was negatively related with adolescents' intention to disclose contact details (Walrave & Heirman, 2013). One recent study investigated how internet tools can be used to protect adolescents from aversive online experiences, such as cyberbullying, being exposed to sexual content and being impersonated (Przybylski & Nash, 2017). Contrary to the study's expectations, no evidence was found that technological tools (such as content filters) reduce adolescents' aversive online experiences.

The abovementioned studies clearly underline that there is a relationship between risk-behaviour and parental media mediation. Empirical research with regard to sexual risk behaviour among adolescents is less conclusive (Ethier, Harper, Hoo, & Dittus, 2016). This might be attributed to the sensitive nature of sexual risk behaviours. Within parental styles, an open, autonomy-supportive communication styles often lead to the most desired outcome (Valkenburg et al., 2013). However, communicating openly about sexting and sexual risk-taking behaviour might be difficult within the family environment. Adolescents tend to avoid discussion about certain topics towards their parents, including their dating experiences (Marshall, Tilton-Weaver, & Bosdet, 2005). Generally, children and adolescents experience talking about sexual topics with their parents as embarrassing (Gunter, 2014). In addition, adolescents believe that their parents should not intervene in their personal relationships with peers (Melotti, Potì, Gianesini, & Brighi, 2017). Mostly, researchers agree that warm and supportive parenting is crucial for a positive parent-child relationship and amount of information that adolescents are willing to disclose to their parents (Melotti et al., 2017). Despite that parental communication about sex is a sensitive topic, parenting has been found to have a significant effect on adolescents' sexual and romantic relationships (Kerpelman, McElwain, Pittman, & Adler-Baeder, 2016).

Miller (2002) reviewed several studies that empirically investigating the relationship between parenting and sexual risk behaviour. One returning finding in studies on family and relationships is that parental warmth is related to lower pregnancy risks by delaying and reducing adolescents sexual intercourse (Miller, 2002). Parent-child closeness is often related to a reduced risk for teenage pregnancies, postponing intercourse, and using contraceptive means (Miller, 2002). Parental control also has been found to impact upon adolescents' sexual behaviour, such as the age of first intercourse, the number of sexual partners, however, overly controlling lead to a higher risk of adolescent pregnancy (Miller, 2002). More recently, Parker and colleagues (Parkes, Henderson, Wight, & Nixon, 2011) investigated among 1990 adolescents whether parenting styles are associated with early sexual risk taking. The results indeed showed a relationship between parenting and delayed intercourse, greater condom use and the increased likelihood that sex occurred within a relationship. The frequency of parental communication about sex was generally low and was less for inexperienced adolescents (i.e. adolescents that had not experienced their first intercourse). However, inexperienced adolescents did report a higher level of supportive parenting. Further, a positive relationship was found between the ease of communication between the parents and the adolescents about adolescents sexual relationships and the first intercourse. In other words, when adolescents feel comfortable to talk about sex with their parents, they are more inclined to delay their first intercourse (Parkes et al., 2011). These results underline the importance of the quality of communication on sexual risk-taking experiences. In a study among 680 adolescents (aged 14–20), adolescents reporting a higher parental psychological report were also more likely to report sexual risk behaviour (Kerpelman et al., 2016).

Sexting is an example of an online sexual risk behaviour (Baumgartner et al., 2012). As mentioned above, only a limited number of studies have touched upon the subject of sexting and parenting. This is surprising as, next to educators, parents are often perceived as important agents to discourage adolescents from sexting behaviour (Draper, 2012). A four-wave panel study among 10,990 adolescents (aged 12–18) found that adolescents who are more susceptible to online and offline risk behaviour (including sexting) are more likely to come from a less cohesive family (Baumgartner et al., 2012). In a study including 25,142 children aged 9–16, Haddon, Loos and Mante-Meijer (Haddon et al., 2012) established 21% of their parents acknowledge that their child had ever received a sexting message. In addition, a significant amount of parents (27%) could not tell whether their child has ever received a sexting message. This indicates that parents are often unaware of what risks children come across online. This lack of awareness may also be attributed to the fact that children do not want to talk with their parents about these risks (Haddon et al., 2012). A telephone-based survey amongst 800 adolescents (aged 12–17 years old) investigated whether children's degree of control or autonomy over their technology use can also be associated with sexting behaviour. In this study, insufficient evidence was found to support this claim. The researchers conclude that restrictive measures are not effective to lower sexting behaviour (Campbell & Park, 2014), which is consistent with above-mentioned parental mediation theories. An important part of parental mediation is also the use of technological tools to shield their children from online risk (behaviour). Houck et al. (2014) touched upon the subject of parental sexual communication and sexting by investigating the relationship between adolescents perceived parental approval for sexual behaviour. In this study, 420 participants between 12 and 14 years old were included, all with previously reported behaviour or emotional problems. This study found that children who sext were more likely to feel that their parents approve their sexual behaviour (Houck et al., 2014).

Conclusion and Recommendations for Future Research

Parents often receive the advice to monitor children's digital behaviour to prevent sexting behaviour (Draper, 2012). However, our literature review suggests that parents could impact upon their children's sexting behaviour in other ways. Parents should play a role in educating their children about sexting. This also applies to parents of adolescents. During adolescence, a time in which sexual experimentation increases, parents should still maintain this supportive role (Ringrose, Gill, Livingstone, & Harvey, 2012). Adolescents should be made aware of the consequences of sexting, how to maintain a normal relationship and the relationship between sexting and other (sexual) risk-taking behaviour (Houck et al., 2014).

Given that parental styles have been found important in numerous online behaviours, the question arises which parental mediation method parents should adopt. Surprisingly, empirical research on parental styles and parental mediation and sexting is currently limited. A majority of these studies do not focus on sexting as the main research topic (Baumgartner et al., 2012; Haddon et al., 2012; Houck et al., 2014; Przybylski & Nash, 2017). Following the SDT and the perceived media mediation theories, parents should communicate about sexting to their adolescents using an autonomy-supportive, non-controlling style. An open communication with regard to general sexual topics is also important (Ringrose et al., 2012). Further, not only frequency of communication is important, but also the ease of the parental communication when it comes to sexual risk behaviour (Parkes et al., 2011). In other words, children and adolescents should be encouraged to speak openly about sexual (risk) behaviour. A crucial aspect is that parents keep the perspective of their child into account (Soenens et al., 2009). This should lead to a better internalization of rules. It is important to emphasise that autonomy-supportive parenting is not a synonym to laissez-faire parenting (Soenens et al., 2009). Even controlling parenting (i.e. setting rules for media use) can be communicated in an autonomy-supportive way. Further research should investigate whether the parental (mediation) styles impact upon sexting behaviour. Moreover, most studies focus on the impact of parental mediation on the prevalence of sexting behaviour. Future research should thoroughly investigate whether parental communication can assist children to deal with negative effects from sexting behaviour.

Shielding adolescents from the Internet is not desirable, as adolescents should learn how to behave responsible online. As mentioned above, overly controlling adolescents' internet behaviour might lead to reactance behaviour. Further, adolescents may even be afraid to share sexting experiences with their parents, because they are afraid for consequences. Research on cyberbullying established that children are often reluctant to share experiences of cyberbullying with their parents, as they are afraid that their parents might restrict their access to technology (Agatston, Kowalski, & Limber, 2012). This might also be the case for sexting behaviour. Instead of trying to shield of their children, parents could also empower their children in using technology to protect them from sexting (consequences). For instance, parents could show their children how to report unwanted contacts, and how to use their privacy settings (Ringrose et al., 2012).

Abovementioned assumptions are primarily based on theoretical insights. Therefore, future research should investigate whether these assumptions hold for sexting and parental styles. This type of research is necessary to provide parents with clear guidelines on how to deal with sexting. Research could also investigate how peer influence and parental influence interact with regard to sexting behaviour. With regard to risk behaviour, peers and friends differ in their type of influence. While friends are more likely to encourage adolescents to test the boundaries of media use, parents try to restrict adolescents from risky behaviour (Sasson & Mesch, 2014). In addition, research should also investigate which role parents can play when sexting behaviour becomes problematic, such as a sexting message being used for cyberbullying. Finally, parents are reluctant to intervene in the personal domain (Smetana & Daddis, 2002) and children are not inclined to discuss sexual aspects with their parents. This may have a major impact on parental communication towards sexting. Future research should investigate how to make sexting a subject open to discussion within the family environment. Discussing the consequences of sexting should be an important part of adolescents' education (Walrave et al., 2015). Parents are major socialization agents, even for adolescents. Investigating how parents can assist their children to cope with sexting behaviour can help children to avoid and deal with unwanted effects after sexting behaviour.

REFERENCES

Agatston, P., Kowalski, R., & Limber, S. (2012). Youth views on cyberbullying. *Cyberbullying Prevention and Response: Expert Perspectives*, 57–71.

Amato, P. R., Meyers, C. E., & Emery, R. E. (2009). Changes in nonresident father-child contact from 1976 to 2002. *Family Relations, 58*(1), 41–53. https://doi.org/10.1111/j.1741-3729.2008.00533.x.

Barber, B. K. (1996). Parental psychological control: Revisiting a neglected construct. *Child Development, 67*(6), 3296–3319.

Bastaits, K., Pasteels, I., Ponnet, K., & Mortelmans, D. (2015). Adult non-response bias from a child perspective. Using child reports to estimate father's non-response. *Social Science Research, 49*, 31–41. https://doi.org/10.1016/j.ssresearch.2014.07.004.

Baumgartner, S. E., Sumter, S. R., Peter, J., & Valkenburg, P. M. (2012). Identifying teens at risk: Developmental pathways of online and offline sexual risk behavior. *Pediatrics, 130*(6), e1489–e1496.

Baumrind, D. (1991). The influence of parenting style on adolescent competence and substance use. *The Journal of Early Adolescence, 11*(1), 56–95.

Borca, G., Bina, M., Keller, P. S., Gilbert, L. R., & Begotti, T. (2015). Internet use and developmental tasks: Adolescents' point of view. *Computers in Human Behavior, 52*, 49–58.

Brehm, J. W. (1966). *A theory of psychological reactance.* New York: Academic.

Buijzen, M., Rozendaal, E., Moorman, M., & Tanis, M. (2008). Parent versus child reports of parental advertising mediation: Exploring the meaning of agreement. *Journal of Broadcasting & Electronic Media, 52*(4), 509–525.

Campbell, S. W., & Park, Y. J. (2014). Predictors of mobile sexting among teens: Toward a new explanatory framework. *Mobile Media & Communication, 2*(1), 20–39.

Choi, H., Van Ouytsel, J., & Temple, J. R. (2016). Association between sexting and sexual coercion among female adolescents. *Journal of Adolescence, 53*, 164–168.

Darling, N., & Steinberg, L. (1993). Parenting style as context. An integrative model. *Psychological Bulletin, 113*(3), 487–496.

Deci, E. L., & Ryan, R. M. (2000). The "what" and "why" of goal pursuits: Human needs and the self-determination of behavior. *Psychological Inquiry, 11*(4), 227–268.

Domenech Rodriguez, M. M., Donovick, M. R., & Crowley, S. L. (2009). Parenting styles in a cultural context: Observations of "protective parenting" in first-generation Latinos. *Family Process, 48*(2), 195–210.

Draper, N. R. A. (2012). Is your teen at risk? Discourses of adolescent sexting in United States television news. *Journal of Children and Media, 6*(2), 221–236. https://doi.org/10.1080/17482798.2011.587147.

Eastin, M. S., Greenberg, B. S., & Hofschire, L. (2006). Parenting the internet. *Journal of Communication, 56*(3), 486–504.

Endendijk, J. J., Groeneveld, M. G., Bakermans-Kranenburg, M. J., & Mesman, J. (2016). Gender-differentiated parenting revisited: Meta-analysis reveals very few differences in parental control of boys and girls. *PLoS One, 11*(7), e0159193.

Ethier, K. A., Harper, C. R., Hoo, E., & Dittus, P. J. (2016). The longitudinal impact of perceptions of parental monitoring on adolescent initiation of sexual activity. *Journal of Adolescent Health, 59*(5), 570–576.

Guay, F., Ratelle, C. F., & Chanal, J. (2008). Optimal learning in optimal contexts: The role of self-determination in education. *Canadian Psychology/Psychologie Canadienne, 49*(3), 233.

Gunter, B. (2014). *Media and the sexualization of childhood.* London, UK: Routledge.

Haddon, L., Loos, E., Haddon, L., & Mante-Meijer, E. (2012). Parental mediation of internet use: Evaluating family relationships. In *Generational use of new media* (pp. 13–30). London, UK: Routledge.

Houck, C. D., Barker, D., Rizzo, C., Hancock, E., Norton, A., & Brown, L. K. (2014). Sexting and sexual behavior in at-risk adolescents. *Pediatrics, 133*(2), e276–e282.

Johnston, H. (2016). Protecting youth's right to engage media: Sexting. In *Adolescents, rapid social change, and the law* (pp. 93–105). Cham, Switzerland: Springer.

Kerpelman, J. L., McElwain, A. D., Pittman, J. F., & Adler-Baeder, F. M. (2016). Engagement in risky sexual behavior: Adolescents' perceptions of self and the parent–child relationship matter. *Youth & Society, 48*(1), 101–125.

Kocayörük, E., Uzman, E., & Mert, A. (2014). How the attachment styles associated with student alienation: The mediation role of emotional well-being. *International Journal of Progressive Education, 10*(3), 34–46.

Kochanska, G., Barry, R. A., Stellern, S. A., & O'Bleness, J. J. (2009). Early attachment organization moderates the parent–child mutually coercive pathway to children's antisocial conduct. *Child Development, 80*(4), 1288–1300.

Lamb, M. (2010). How do father influence children's development? Let me count the ways. In M. Lamb (Ed.), *The role of the father in child development* (5th ed., pp. 1–26). Hoboken, NJ: Wiley.

Lau, W. W., & Yuen, A. H. (2013). Adolescents' risky online behaviours: The influence of gender, religion, and parenting style. *Computers in Human Behavior, 29*(6), 2690–2696.

Livingstone, S. (2007). Strategies of parental regulation in the media-rich home. *Computers in Human Behavior, 23*(2), 920–941.

Livingstone, S., & Helsper, E. (2007). Gradations in digital inclusion: Children, young people and the digital divide. *New Media & Society, 9*(4), 671–696.

Lwin, M. O., Stanaland, A. J., & Miyazaki, A. D. (2008). Protecting children's privacy online: How parental mediation strategies affect website safeguard effectiveness. *Journal of Retailing, 84*(2), 205–217.

Mandara, J., Murray, C. B., Telesford, J. M., Varner, F. A., & Richman, S. B. (2012). Observed gender differences in African American mother-child relationships and child behavior. *Family Relations, 61*(1), 129–141.

Marshall, S. K., Tilton-Weaver, L. C., & Bosdet, L. (2005). Information management: Considering adolescents' regulation of parental knowledge. *Journal of Adolescence, 28*(5), 633–647.

McKinney, C., & Renk, K. (2008). Differential parenting between mothers and fathers: Implications for late adolescents. *Journal of Family Issues, 29*(6), 806–827.

Melotti, G., Potì, S., Gianesini, G., & Brighi, A. (2017). Adolescents at risk of delinquency. The role of parental control, trust, and disclosure. *Deviant Behavior*, 1–16.

Miller, B. C. (2002). Family influences on adolescent sexual and contraceptive behavior. *Journal of Sex Research, 39*(1), 22–26.

Nathanson, A. I. (2001). Parent and child perspectives on the presence and meaning of parental television mediation. *Journal of Broadcasting & Electronic Media, 45*(2), 201–220.

Otten, R., Engels, R. C., van de Ven, M. O., & Bricker, J. B. (2007). Parental smoking and adolescent smoking stages: The role of parents' current and former smoking, and family structure. *Journal of Behavioral Medicine, 30*(2), 143–154.

Parkes, A., Henderson, M., Wight, D., & Nixon, C. (2011). Is parenting associated with teenagers' early sexual risk-taking, autonomy and relationship with sexual partners? *Perspectives on Sexual and Reproductive Health, 43*(1), 30–40.

Phares, V., Fields, S., & Kamboukos, D. (2009). Fathers' and mothers' involvement with their adolescents. *Journal of Child and Family Studies, 18*(1), 1–9.

Przybylski, A. K., & Nash, V. (2017). Internet filtering technology and aversive online experiences in adolescents. *The Journal of Pediatrics, 184,* 215–219. e211.

Ringrose, J., Gill, R., Livingstone, S., & Harvey, L. (2012). *A qualitative study of children, young people and 'sexting'*. A report prepared for the NSPCC.

Rosen, L. D., Cheever, N. A., & Carrier, L. M. (2008). The association of parenting style and child age with parental limit setting and adolescent MySpace behavior. *Journal of Applied Developmental Psychology, 29*(6), 459–471.

Sasson, H., & Mesch, G. (2014). Parental mediation, peer norms and risky online behavior among adolescents. *Computers in Human Behavior, 33,* 32–38.

Shin, W., Huh, J., & Faber, R. J. (2012). Tweens' online privacy risks and the role of parental mediation. *Journal of Broadcasting & Electronic Media, 56*(4), 632–649.

Shin, W., & Ismail, N. (2014). Exploring the role of parents and peers in young adolescents' risk taking on social networking sites. *Cyberpsychology, Behavior, and Social Networking, 17*(9), 578–583.

Smetana, J. G., & Daddis, C. (2002). Domain-specific antecedents of parental psychological control and monitoring: The role of parenting beliefs and practices. *Child Development, 73*(2), 563–580.

Sneegas, J. E., & Plank, T. A. (1998). Gender differences in pre-adolescent reactance to age-categorized television advisory labels. *Journal of Broadcasting & Electronic Media, 42*(4), 423–434.

Soenens, B., & Vansteenkiste, M. (2010). A theoretical upgrade of the concept of parental psychological control: Proposing new insights on the basis of self-determination theory. *Developmental Review, 30*(1), 74–99.

Soenens, B., Vansteenkiste, M., & Niemiec, C. P. (2009). Should parental prohibition of adolescents' peer relationships be prohibited? *Personal Relationships, 16*(4), 507–530.

Stattin, H., & Kerr, M. (2000). Parental monitoring: A reinterpretation. *Child Development, 71*(4), 1072–1085.

Symons, K., Ponnet, K., Emmery, K., Walrave, M., & Heirman, W. (2017). Parental knowledge of adolescents' online content and contact risks. *Journal of Youth and Adolescence, 46*(2), 401–416.

Tamis-LeMonda, C. S., Briggs, R. D., McClowry, S. G., & Snow, D. L. (2009). Maternal control and sensitivity, child gender, and maternal education in relation to children's behavioral outcomes in African American families. *Journal of Applied Developmental Psychology, 30*(3), 321–331.

Temple, J. R., Le, V. D., van den Berg, P., Ling, Y., Paul, J. A., & Temple, B. W. (2014). Brief report: Teen sexting and psychosocial health. *Journal of Adolescence, 37*(1), 33–36.

Valcke, M., Bonte, S., De Wever, B., & Rots, I. (2010). Internet parenting styles and the impact on internet use of primary school children. *Computers & Education, 55*(2), 454–464.

Valkenburg, P. M., Krcmar, M., Peeters, A. L., & Marseille, N. M. (1999). Developing a scale to assess three styles of television mediation: "Instructive mediation," "restrictive mediation," and "social coviewing". *Journal of Broadcasting & Electronic Media, 43*(1), 52–66.

Valkenburg, P. M., Piotrowski, J. T., Hermanns, J., & Leeuw, R. (2013). Developing and validating the perceived parental media mediation scale: A self-determination perspective. *Human Communication Research, 39*(4), 445–469.

Van Ouytsel, J., Ponnet, K., & Walrave, M. (2016). Cyber dating abuse victimization among secondary school students from a lifestyle-routine activities theory perspective. *Journal of Interpersonal Violence*, pii: 0886260516629390.

Vanhaelewyn, B., & De Marez, L. (2016). *Digimeter 2016 – Measuring digital trends in Flanders.* Retrieved from http://eproofing.springer.com/books/index.php?token=irMdoBsimvhrTXbdxaueAziN1J5nLmRUOuRr0c9ehqY

Walrave, M., & Heirman, W. (2013). Adolescents, online marketing and privacy: Predicting adolescents' willingness to disclose personal information for marketing purposes. *Children & Society, 27*(6), 434–447.

Walrave, M., Ponnet, K., Van Ouytsel, J., Van Gool, E., Heirman, W., & Verbeek, A. (2015). Whether or not to engage in sexting: Explaining adolescent sexting behaviour by applying the prototype willingness model. *Telematics and Informatics, 32*(4), 796–808.

Walsh, A. D., Laczniak, R. N., & Carlson, L. (1998). Mothers' preferences for regulating children's television. *Journal of Advertising, 27*(3), 23–36.

Warren, R. (2001). In words and deeds: Parental involvement and mediation of children's television viewing. *The Journal of Family Communication, 1*(4), 211–231.

Woodworth, S., Belsky, J., & Crnic, K. (1996). The determinants of fathering during the child's second and third years of life: A developmental analysis. *Journal of Marriage and the Family, 58*(3), 679–692.

Yardi, S., & Bruckman, A. (2011). *Social and technical challenges in parenting teens' social media use.* Paper presented at the proceedings of the SIGCHI conference on human factors in computing systems. Vancouver, BC, Canada.

CHAPTER 6

Slut-Shaming 2.0

Kathleen Van Royen, Karolien Poels, Heidi Vandebosch,
and Michel Walrave

Abstract The practice of slut-shaming became rampant with the advent of social networking sites (SNS). This chapter will discuss how these platforms pose additional risks for female adolescents to be slut-shamed. It will be argued that SNS have expanded the impact and scope of slut-shaming through, for example, the easy replication and persistence of publicly visible content on SNS. Furthermore, this chapter will examine the prevalence and characteristics of slut-shaming (derived from perceptions of the victim's point of view) particularly on SNS, based on a survey study amongst 476 adolescent females (12–18 years). To conclude, efforts will be discussed to prevent this form of harassment. Several actors such as parents, schools, mass media and social media providers, should take more responsibility as well as convey equal gender norms starting from a young age.

Keywords Adolescents • Social networking sites • Slut-shaming • Prevalence • Characteristics

K. Van Royen (✉) • K. Poels • H. Vandebosch • M. Walrave
Department of Communication Studies, MIOS, University of Antwerp,
Antwerp, Belgium

© The Author(s) 2018
M. Walrave et al. (eds.), *Sexting*, Palgrave Studies in Cyberpsychology,
https://doi.org/10.1007/978-3-319-71882-8_6

SLUT-SHAMING

Slut-shaming is the act of attacking a female for perceived or real sexual activity by calling her a slut or similar names (Papp et al., 2015). In addition to slut-shaming within schools (Ringrose & Renold, 2010), a setting where female adolescents are labelled as sluts is the online environment, in particular on *social networking sites* (SNS) (Ringrose, 2011). With the rapid rise of social media and their frequent use by adolescents (Lenhart, 2015) it is important to gain a better understanding of the slut shaming phenomenon in a SNS context.

Although terms like 'slut' or 'whore' are often used in a reciprocal way and become increasingly acceptable nicknames among friends in youth, these terms may be used in an unwelcome way and may take the form of harassment or sexualized bullying (Tanenbaum, 2015). Thus, it is important to understand the characteristics of the *'unwelcome'* incidents of slut-shaming (perceived as harassment) in particular. This latter practice is sometimes referred to as 'slut-bashing', which is a 'form of overt bullying intentionally and repeatedly targeted towards a female because she does not adhere to feminine norms' (Tanenbaum, 2015, p. 4). The term 'slut-shaming' is used more diffuse, as a casual form of judgement, not necessarily meant for bullying or harassing. Usually the literature refers to slut-shaming and this concept will also be used as overarching term for both bashing and shaming throughout this paper.

Slut-shaming originates from the still widely held beliefs of the sexual double standard (Kreager & Staff, 2009; Ringrose, Harvey, Gill, & Livingstone, 2013). According to this standard males are rewarded and praised for perceived or real sexual activity, whereas females are condemned for similar behaviours (Crawford & Popp, 2003). Reasons for being slut-shamed include: behaving too sexual or being a victim of sexual assault (Tanenbaum, 2015; Weiss, 2010). However, slut-shaming does not always have to do with individual sexual conduct, but often concerns public gender performances (Armstrong, Hamilton, Armstrong, & Seeley, 2014), in a sense that slut-shamed females are sanctioned for failing to perform femininity in an acceptable way. A female who is different from her peers by violating gendered norms - for instance by demonstrating more agency – may be victimized (Ringrose & Renold, 2010; Tanenbaum, 2015). These feminine norms imply that females are expected to behave according to a 'gender script' demonstrating characteristics such as being nice (i.e. modest, caring etc.) and passive femininity (i.e. being sexually faithful/innocent) (Mahalik et al., 2005; Ringrose & Renold, 2010). Female adolescents slut-shame each other (Armstrong et al., 2014; Poole, 2014), for example to differentiate a specific group of female adolescents as the 'other' and distinct themselves as the 'good' ones (Armstrong et al., 2014; Caron, 2008). This is in line with the *self-esteem hypothesis* suggesting that female adolescents slut-shame others to boost their own self-esteem (Clayton & Trafimow, 2007; Papp et al., 2015). Another important motivation for female adolescents is an expression of envy towards a pretty female, as slut-shaming makes the harasser feel more powerful and helps to win male approval by raising herself up in the hierarchy (Poole, 2014; Tanenbaum, 2015). This is based on the idea of the *competition hypothesis*, in which adolescents view other females as competitors for the most desirable males (Clayton & Trafimow, 2007; Papp et al., 2015). It is less understood why male adolescents harass, but it is argued that those males position themselves to the 'slut' in order to reinforce their own masculinity and to control women's sexuality (Papp et al., 2015). Controlling a woman's sexuality, i.e. preventing her from having other sexual experiences and being faithful, is an important source of male pride and status (Rudman, Fetterolf, & Sanchez, 2013). Another hypothesis may be that men who are concerned about women's infidelity, may express their jealousy through slut-shaming (Baumeister & Twenge, 2002; Papp et al., 2015). Sexual harassment and slut-shaming, in particular by males, is said to be a way 'to express and reconfirm the public and private positions of hegemonic masculinity within a heterosexualized gender order' (Robinson, 2005, p. 20). In this light, slut-shaming by males can be considered as a means to maintain and regulate hierarchical power relationships (Robinson, 2005).

Gendered Representations on SNS

The practice of slut-shaming became even more rampant with the advent of social media. Adolescents are extremely active on these platforms, with 71% of them using more than one SNS (Lenhart, 2015). These platforms pose additional risks for a female adolescent to be slut-shamed. SNS allow adolescents to participate through producing self-representations, often presenting themselves in a gendered stereotypical manner (Bailey, Steeves, Burkell, & Regan, 2013; Carstensen, 2009; Kapidzic & Herring, 2011). Males tend to portray themselves on SNS according to norms of masculinity in which they embody strength and power (Manago, Graham,

Greenfield, & Salimkhan, 2008). Females often emphasize their physical beauty and present themselves as sexually available and eager to please males (Kapidzic & Herring, 2011). Along with the opportunity of social status rewards for this online self-exposure, comes the risk of harsh judgments (Bailey et al., 2013). Female adolescents have to constantly negotiate between presenting themselves as sexy but not too sexy (Poole, 2014; Ringrose, Gill, Livingstone, & Harvey, 2012). This consideration also has to be made in regard with sexting, defined as the interpersonal transmission of sexually provocative or suggestive (nearly) nude images through digital technologies (Döring, 2014; Lenhart, 2009). Female adolescents perceive on the one hand, particularly from males, a social pressure to 'sext' since by not doing so, they may be labelled as 'prude' or 'stuck up' (Lippman & Campbell, 2014). However, at the same time, female adolescents engaging in sexting, may be morally sanctioned through slut-shaming (Lippman & Campbell, 2014; Ringrose et al., 2013).

SNS have expanded the occurrence and impact of slut-shaming (Poole, 2014). The highly interactive nature of SNS contributes to the maintenance and escalation of these behaviours (Barak, 2005). Interactive messages usually contain more expressions of agreement which consequently can reinforce the message (Rafaeli & Sudweeks, 1997). The specific design of SNS contributes to the nature of risks. boyd (2008) identifies features such as 'persistence' (content remains online), 'searchability' (easy retrievable content), 'replicability' (possibility of copying the same message) and 'invisible audiences' (the lack of certainty about who receives any communication). These features of SNS may increase the impact, for example persistence and searchability extend the period of existence of the content (boyd, 2008). At the same time, easy replication of the content can result in a higher degree of forwarding and thus more harassers could become involved. Furthermore, publicly visible content may increase the severity since others might replicate and forward the harassing content (Sticca & Perren, 2012).

Prevalence and Characteristics of Online Slut-Shaming

It has been reported that women who are being slut-shamed are facing damaged self-perceptions and psychological harms (Poole, 2014). Several individual consequences of slut-shaming have been documented, including less peer acceptance (Kreager & Staff, 2009) and various negative outcomes for physical and mental health (Tanenbaum, 2015). Moreover, slut-shaming has various societal impacts through encouraging gender inequality and sustaining the sexual double standard, which ultimately may result in the acceptance of sexual harassment (Tanenbaum, 2015).

Scarce academic research has been devoted to online slut-shaming, as this practice is often investigated under the umbrella of bullying (boyd, 2014; Papp et al., 2015; Poole, 2014). Nevertheless, several authors have reported on slut-shaming practices occurring on SNS based on interviews or on news media coverage (Poole, 2014; Ringrose, 2011; Ringrose et al., 2013; Tanenbaum, 2015). Although these cases allow us to gain further insight in the occurrence of slut-shaming, to the best of our knowledge, no empirical data are available regarding its prevalence. In general, the AAUW (American Association of University Women) found that 17% of the female adolescents had unwelcome sexual rumours spread about them online (Hill & Kearl, 2011). Our first research question (RQ1) seeks to provide data on how many female adolescents are being slut-shamed on SNS and who these victims are in terms of age, education type and exposure to unwanted sexual comments offline. Previous reports suggest that older adolescents are more exposed to sexual messages online than younger adolescents (Baumgartner, Valkenburg, & Peter, 2010; Ybarra & Mitchell, 2008). However, from a sexual developmental perspective (Moore & Rosenthal, 2006), we might expect that early adolescents are more likely to be morally sanctioned for perceived or real sexual conduct in comparison with the elder ones. In addition, we investigate whether this name-calling solely occurs online or whether these females at the same time receive unwanted sexual comments offline. In general, it is said that encountering more offline risks is related to higher online risks (Baumgartner, Sumter, Peter, & Valkenburg, 2012).

Situational characteristics (e.g. multiple perpetrators, power imbalance) play a role in the impact of harassment (Mitchell, Ybarra, Jones, & Espelage, 2014). Those characteristics can give us a better understanding of the context of unwelcome slut-shaming incidents, such as the relationship between harasser(s) and victim, whether it is a public or a private attack, who the harassers are in terms of demographics and how the victimized females perceive this event themselves. Our second research question (RQ2) will provide an answer to questions regarding the characteristics of slut-shaming events on SNS and reasons for being slut-shamed. By allowing victims to describe the event in their own words, we gain insight in reasons why they consider themselves to be slut-shamed and what they perceive as important in this event, which may inspire preventive actions.

METHODS

Participants and Procedures

A questionnaire was administered among female adolescents, aged between 12 and 18 years old, from 11 secondary schools in Flanders (*n* = 476 (*M* age = 15.04; *SD* = 1.87)) in 2014. This study was framed within a larger purpose to examine gender-based harassment of Flemish adolescents via social media. Classes within schools were sampled based on a stratified convenience sampling method. The sampling criteria were grade and education type. Grades were 1st grade (1st and 2nd year of secondary school; 29.2%), 2nd grade (3rd and 4th year; 39.2%) and 3rd grade (5th and 6th year; 31.6%). Education types included general education (43.2%), vocational (32.6%) and technical education (24.2%). Data were weighted to obtain a representative sample.

After obtaining consent from the school principal, passive informed consent was obtained from parents. Prior to completion of the questionnaires, adolescents were introduced to the procedure and study purposes and were asked to give active consent by signing the form. This study protocol received ethical approval from the University Ethical Advisory Committee for Social and Human Sciences.

Description of Measures

First, participants were asked to provide *demographic information* including their age and education type. *Online slut-shaming* was measured by asking the participants how frequently they had been called slut, whore or similar names in the past six months on SNS while perceiving this as 'unwelcome' (5 categories ranging from 'Never' to 'Few times per week', with values from 0 to 4). Other forms of online gender-based harassment (e.g. receiving comments related to looks or body) were measured in the same way.

In addition, participants were asked to indicate the frequency of *receiving unwanted sexual comments in real life* in the past six months (five categories ranging from 'Never' to 'Every day'). This was defined as: 'unwelcome sexual comments, jokes or gestures in real life.'

As we included other gender-based harassment forms in our survey, we asked female adolescents to mark the worst situation of gender-based harassment they received to further solicit the specific situational characteristics of one incident. Therefore, measures of all next variables are only available for those who indicated an online slut-shaming event to be the worst situation they had encountered. Questions were asked about *several situational characteristics of the event*, such as the SNS platform on which it occurred (e.g. Facebook), the location of the situation (e.g. public page, profile page), the gender of the harasser(s), whether the harasser was below 18 years old, if there were multiple harassers involved and the relation to the harasser(s) (e.g. friend in real life). Next, participants were asked to briefly describe the incident in their own words (open-ended question).

Data Analysis Strategy

In regard with the first aim of our study, we generated descriptive statistics on the prevalence of slut-shaming victimization on SNS, the characteristics of the victims, and for the situational characteristics of the event.

To analyse the qualitative data based on the answers of the open-ended question in which participants were asked to provide a brief description of the event, a thematic analysis was used. All answers were coded in Nvivo by linking these to themes and searching recurring patterns in the answers. The codebook was based on existing literature regarding reasons for being slut-shamed for example 'sexual double standard', 'jealousy', 'violating gendered norms' (Armstrong et al., 2014; Baumeister & Twenge, 2002; Clayton & Trafimow, 2007; Papp et al., 2015; Ringrose & Renold, 2010). These existing categories were used as sensitizing concepts in the analysis, offering guidance for developing thematic categories from the data (Bowen, 2006). The final number of categories was 13, including categories such as jealousy, sexual double standard, common insulting language, but also 'undetermined' (see for more categories under section 'Brief Descriptions of the Event by Victimized Female Adolescents'). Afterwards, a second coder independently reviewed the codes (Kappa = 0.743 with $p < .001$) and where disagreement was found, this was discussed.

RESULTS

Prevalence of Slut-Shaming on SNS

Who Was the Victim? In total 18.7% ($n = 84$) of the female adolescents in our sample was at least once slut-shamed on SNS in the past six months

Table 6.1 Frequency of slut-shaming on SNS

Frequency in the past six months	% (n)
Never	81.3 (363)
Once	8.4 (37)
A few times	5.4 (24)
Once per month	1.8 (8)
A few times per month	1.3 (6)
A few times per week	1.9 (9)
Missing	29

preceding the survey and perceived this as harassing (i.e. unwelcome) (see Table 6.1 for all frequencies). 10.4% of our sample did not just experience this once but at least a few times in this six months. Among the slut-shamed victims, 80.7% perceived this incident as severe, whereas 19.3% did not.

The average age of the victimized females was 15.04 ($SD = 1.92$). Among the group of 12 to 14 year olds ($n = 162$), 21% was slut-shamed ($n = 34$). Among females aged between 15 and 18 years old ($n = 285$), 17.5% was at least once named a slut ($n = 50$). However, this difference was not statistically significant ($\chi^2 = .803$; $p > .05$). In vocational education ($n = 105$) 31.4% ($n = 33$) was being slut-shamed at least once, which was significantly ($\chi^2 = 14.36$; $p < .05$) more than those from other educational levels ($n = 342$) (general and technical). Among the latter in total 14.9% ($n = 51$) had been slut-shamed on SNS. Furthermore, slut-shaming on SNS was correlated with receiving unwanted sexual comments offline ($r = .340$; $p < .001$). Among the victims, 91.5% also received at least once a sexually harassing comment in the past six months in real life.

Next, we asked victims to describe one event, which they perceived as the most severe among other gender-based harassment forms (e.g. homophobic comments) on SNS they were solicited about. From the 84 slut-shamed adolescents in our sample, 46 female adolescents marked slut-shaming as the worst incident out of the harassment forms on SNS they encountered. These 46 female adolescents were further solicited about the characteristics of the incident and their experienced emotions. For eight out of these 46 female adolescents, slut-shaming was the only form of gender-based harassment they encountered on SNS.

Situational Characteristics of the Most Severe Slut-Shaming Incidents on SNS

Where Did It Happen? The platform on which the incidents of slut-shaming occurred most frequently was Facebook (75%) as this is also the platform that is used mostly among the adolescents (94.7% of the victims had a Facebook profile). In the second place, female adolescents were slut-shamed on Ask.fm (25.8%). Instagram accounted for 5%.

Most often the female was victimized via a private way (chat or message) (56.9%). All other cases were publicly visible (43.1%). Of the latter 14.2% occurred as a comment on a picture or profile (which is by default publicly visible, but may have been changed in the privacy settings).

Who Was the Harasser? In more than half of the events (53.3%) multiple harassers were involved in slut-shaming on SNS, whereas in 24% there was only one harasser and 22.7% of the victims did not know the number of harassers.

Harassers were most often someone they knew, such as friends in real life (39.6%) or an acquaintance (16.9%). However, victims were also often slut-shamed by someone whose name was visible but unknown to the victim (25.5%). Other harassers were anonymous (no name visible) (22%), someone only known through the internet (4.8%), or someone else (4.1%). The total percentage here is more than 100%, as in case of multiple harassers some respondents indicated more categories.

Most often the harasser was a boy (36.7%), or both girls and boys (25.5%) were involved. In 14.5% of the cases the act was conducted by (a) female(s). In almost one fourth of the incidents (23.3%) the victim did not know the gender of the harasser(s).

In several cases, the harasser was older than 18 years old (14.4%), but most often it was a minor (55.5%), whereas often it was not known how old the harasser was (30.1%) (for instance, when the harasser acted anonymously).

Brief Descriptions of the Event by Victimized Female Adolescents

Female adolescents who were victimized through online slut-shaming were solicited to recall and briefly describe the most severe event (or the only event encountered).

Descriptions of the event often clearly indicated a feeling of *jealousy* from (an)other female(s) towards the victim. For example, someone said: 'A female had called me a slut several times because I had kissed a boy with whom she is having a relationship with but this happened before they were a couple' (17 years old). Slut-shaming by boys was sometimes motivated by attempts to *reinforce their masculinity* when they felt threatened or jealous. Some female adolescents referred in their description of the event to this practice: 'Someone called me a whore, because he could not get me' (16 years old).

Descriptions demonstrate that online slut-shaming not only concerns the moral sanctioning of online behaviour but also of offline behaviour that is perceived *as a violation of gender norms*. Victimized female adolescents often referred to offline sexualized behaviour as a reason for being called a slut, and not only sexually suggestive representations online: 'I was called slut because I was wearing a revealing top when it was hot at school' (13 years old). Also reasons such as *being different from others* were observed, for example because of attention deficit hyperactivity disorder (ADHD) or after an abortion. Furthermore, this occurred as a *consequence of offline sexual victimization* as a female commented to have been slut-shamed after being raped.

Some female adolescents referred to the violated gender norms in the form of the *sexual double standard*: 'If you post a picture online with a boy that is not your boyfriend, then you are immediately being called a whore or slut.' (18 years old). One respondent indicated that girls are always the 'bad' ones compared to boys: 'Someone's boyfriend wanted to be with me [in a relationship], but I was the slut.' (18 years old).

Moreover, some descriptions indicated that online slut-shaming has become *common insulting language* used in the context of a fight: 'An old friend with whom I had a quarrel for years, had started a group page on Facebook against me and made Facebook pages on which she breaks me down, insults me' (17 years old). Often these names are used without meaning as insults in quarrels. In line with this, several victimized female adolescents felt that slut-shaming is *part of daily discourse on SNS and is often used without a valid reason*, according to the female adolescents: 'Nowadays people often call all females a whore, also me' (13 years old). Moreover, the *anonymity on some SNS* facilitates slut-shaming: 'I often received anonymous messages saying that they thought I was a whore, slut, etc.' (14 years old).

Finally, some victimized adolescents *blamed themselves* for being slut-shamed. One respondent said: 'I was called slut due to wrong choices I had made' (16 years old).

DISCUSSION

The present study shows that nearly one in five (18.7%) of the female adolescents was slut-shamed on SNS at least once in the past six months. Moreover, the majority of all victimized female adolescents perceived it as (rather) severe. These results provide empirical evidence to support claims made in previous reports regarding online slut-shaming to engage in actions to prevent this practice (Poole, 2014; Tanenbaum, 2015).

In regard with the profile of the victims, our findings indicate that younger female adolescents did experience slightly more online slut-shaming, but this difference was not found to be significant. Even though late adolescents are more exposed to the risk of receiving sexual messages (Baumgartner et al., 2010; Ybarra & Mitchell, 2008), younger adolescents feel usually more upset and harmed by it (Livingstone & Görzig, 2014; Mitchell, Finkelhor, & Wolak, 2001), which explains we found higher numbers of unwelcome slut-shaming among the latter group. Moreover, female adolescents who were slut-shamed were more likely to be enrolled in vocational education, confirming previous reports on cyberbullying that this is mainly an issue in vocational education levels (Walrave & Heirman, 2011). Finally, we found that victims of online slut-shaming are at the same time more confronted with unwelcome sexual comments offline. Similarly, for cyberbullying there is considerable overlap with traditional bullying (Erdur-Baker, 2010; Ybarra, Diener-West, & Leaf, 2007).

With regard to the situational characteristics of online slut-shaming, we asked the victimized females to think of the most severe incident they experienced in the past six months. We found that these most severe incidents were often performed on the mainstream SNS platform such as Facebook, which may be caused by the feature of this platform that promotes commenting on others' posts. However, also Ask.fm was mentioned quite often, which is an anonymous platform and was previously one of the most used SNS platforms for cyberbullying (Hosseinmardi et al., 2014).

Furthermore, we found that online slut-shaming was most often performed by multiple harassers (in 53.3% of the events). However, this percentage may be high because we asked victims to describe the most severe incident they encountered on SNS and the severity of harassment increases when multiple harassers are involved (Mitchell et al., 2014). Our findings indicate that both males and females engage in practices of slut-shaming. Several authors already mentioned that females are often involved in these acts to compete for male approval and as a way to feel powerful (Clayton & Trafimow, 2007; Papp et al., 2015).

Female adolescents also indicated that they were often slut-shamed by friends in real life (in 39.6%), which may be high since the victims' descriptions concern the most severe case of slut-shaming and they might perceive this as worse than being slut-shamed by strangers. First, this may be explained by the context of reciprocal slut-shaming, in which friends call each other sluts (Ringrose & Barajas, 2011; Tanenbaum, 2015). It may be that female adolescents were called this way by friends for the sake of a joke or to rebel against the victim position associated with these labels (Ringrose & Barajas, 2011) but did perceive it as 'unwelcome'. Often female adolescents' interactions on SNS are characterized by practices such as arguing, jealousy, name-calling or jokes, in which the boundaries between joking versus harm are often blurred (Marwick & boyd, 2011). This may be sometimes misinterpreted by the receiver because nonverbal cues typically lack in the online environment, except for emoticons (Walther & D'Addario, 2001). Second, the occurrence of online slut-shaming between friends in real life can also be explained by the use of these terms in the context of a fight, which was also shown by the qualitative data. Worrisome are the indications that words such as slut are part of daily discourses on SNS, the reciprocal use among friends or using these nicknames for themselves reclaiming the meaning of slut as cool (Ringrose & Barajas, 2011; Ringrose, 2011). Even when these words are used without a malicious intent or in a light-hearted manner, sexist and specious ideas about femininity and the sexual double standard may remain in order (Tanenbaum, 2015). In addition, in this way female adolescents foster their sexual objectification by linking their personal worth to their ability to be sexually attractive (Ringrose, 2011).

Throughout the descriptions of the female adolescents, we found evidence for the motivations behind online slut-shaming as theorized before. For instance, it was found that a male engaged in slut-shaming because 'he could not get her', which can be seen as a way to reinforce his own masculinity and regain power over the female (Papp et al., 2015). In addition, the sexual double standard and sanctioning for the violation of gender norms, was often observed in the descriptions, which confirms the idea of gender imbalance and power, underlying slut-shaming (Tanenbaum, 2015). Moreover, the motivation of jealousy described by the female adolescents, is in line with the competition hypothesis, which states that female adolescents view other female adolescents as competitors for males (Clayton & Trafimow, 2007). Furthermore, the qualitative data show that slut-shaming on SNS is not an isolated phenomenon and often relates to offline incidents as a reason for being called a slut on SNS, and to a less extent solely about sexualized representations in cyberspace (e.g. choosing provocative pictures, sexting). SNS are therefore an additional way to slut-shame female adolescents sometimes already considered as sluts in real life. Furthermore, SNS might increase slut-shaming practices because of the ease and its potential anonymity. This was also indicated by the female adolescents in our sample, who responded that they were often slut-shamed through anonymous messages (22% of the harassers were anonymous).

Implications

In general, since the prevalence rates and perceived severity among slut-shamed female adolescents are fairly high, efforts to reduce this form of harassment are needed. These results implicate that parents (or caretakers) and schools must educate both males and females starting from a young age, not only about online e-safety but also about femininity and equal gender norms. The popular media bear responsibility in the mixed messages they convey about women's sexuality, on the one hand promoting sexualized images of women and on the other hand, stigmatizing women who are assertive in expressing their sexuality (Littleton, 2011). Popular media, particularly in programs for children and adolescents, have an important role in refraining from objectification of women. Moreover, as some female adolescents blamed themselves for what happened, awareness programs aimed at sexting should be re-positioned away from emphasizing victim responsibility and blaming (Döring, 2014; Salter, Crofts, & Lee, 2013). Furthermore, SNS providers have a role in increasing safety measures and providing responses to this practice of slut-shaming on their platforms (Poole, 2014). First, all SNS should emphasize in their community guidelines that gender-based violence is not tolerated. Second, warnings must be used against harassers. For instance, when one is repeatedly engaging in slut-shaming on SNS, this person should receive a message indicating that this behaviour is not tolerated and that eventually sanctions will be taken.

Finally, we need to arm female adolescents with coping and emotion regulation strategies, and how to deal with these situations.

This study has a number of limitations. Due to a lack of a validated scale, we measured slut-shaming with a single item and did not include a response option for being named 'every day' a slut. Future studies could develop and test a more elaborate measure of slut-shaming. Moreover, we used a convenience sampling method for recruiting the respondents in this study. Convenience samples do not always produce representative results, even with a posteriori sampling weighing. Therefore the prevalence rates might be slightly biased and should be interpreted with care.

In addition, this overview of incident characteristics is limited to the most severe incidents that victims experienced. Therefore, results do not reflect the picture for all and less severe online slut-shaming incidents. Second, we do not know why the victims selected these events as the most severe ones. Therefore, future research could investigate the context of the selected event and reasons why they consider it as most severe. The analysis is limited to slut-shamed females. We did not look at characteristics of slut-shamed males. However, literature indicates that also boys are becoming slut-shamed (Skoog & Bayram Özdemir, 2016), demonstrating also sexual standards for men exist (Marks & Fraley, 2005) or even a reverse sexual double standard (Papp et al., 2015).

CONCLUSION

Findings indicate that nearly one fifth of the female adolescents was at least once called 'unwantedly' whore, slut or similar names on SNS in the past six months. Situational characteristics and descriptions by the female adolescents show that slut-shaming on SNS can be encountered in different ways and for several reasons of both offline and online alleged behaviour. Efforts to address online slut-shaming are needed and actors such as parents, schools and (social) media, should take more responsibility as well as convey equal gender norms starting from a young age.

REFERENCES

Armstrong, E. A., Hamilton, L. T., Armstrong, E. M., & Seeley, J. L. (2014). "Good girls" gender, social class, and slut discourse on campus. *Social Psychology Quarterly, 77*(2), 100–122.

Bailey, J., Steeves, V., Burkell, J., & Regan, P. (2013). Negotiating with gender stereotypes on social networking sites: From "bicycle face" to Facebook. *Journal of Communication Inquiry, 37*(2), 91–112.

Barak, A. (2005). Sexual harassment on the internet. *Social Science Computer Review, 23,* 77–92.

Baumeister, R. F., & Twenge, J. M. (2002). Cultural suppression of female sexuality. *Review of General Psychology, 6*(2), 166–203.

Baumgartner, S., Sumter, S., Peter, J., & Valkenburg, P. (2012). Identifying teens at risk: Developmental pathways of online and offline sexual risk behavior. *Pediatrics, 130*(6), e1489–e1496.

Baumgartner, S., Valkenburg, P., & Peter, J. (2010). Unwanted online sexual solicitation and risky sexual online behavior across the lifespan. *Journal of Applied Developmental Psychology, 31*(6), 439–447.

Bowen, G. (2006). Grounded theory and sensitizing concepts. *International Journal of Qualitative Methods, 5*(3), 1–9.

boyd, d. (2008). Why youth (h) social network sites: The role of networked publics in teenage social life. In *Youth, identity, and digital media* (Vol. 6, pp. 119–142). Cambridge, MA: MIT Press.

boyd, d. (2014). *It's complicated: The social lives of networked teens.* New Haven, CT: Yale University Press.

Caron, C. (2008). *Sexy girls as the « Other »: The discursive processes of stigmatizing girls.* Presented at the Canadian Communication Association Conference, University of British Columbia.

Carstensen, T. (2009). Gender trouble in web 2.0. Gender relations in social network sites, wikis and weblogs. *International Journal of Gender, Science and Technology, 1*(1), 106–127.

Clayton, K. D., & Trafimow, D. (2007). A test of three hypotheses concerning attributions toward female promiscuity. *The Social Science Journal, 44*(4), 677–686.

Crawford, M., & Popp, D. (2003). Sexual double standards: A review and methodological critique of two decades of research. *The Journal of Sex Research, 40*(1), 13–26.

Döring, N. (2014). Consensual sexting among adolescents: Risk prevention through abstinence education or safer sexting? *Cyberpsychology: Journal of Psychosocial Research on Cyberspace, 8*(1), article 9.

Erdur-Baker, Ö. (2010). Cyberbullying and its correlation to traditional bullying, gender and frequent and risky usage of internet-mediated communication tools. *New Media & Society, 12*(1), 109–125.

Hill, C., & Kearl, H. (2011). *Crossing the line: Sexual harassment at school* (p. 444). Washington, DC: American Association of University Women (AAUW).

Hosseinmardi, H., Rafiq, R. I., Li, S., Yang, Z., Han, R., Mishra, S., & Lv, Q. (2014). *A comparison of common users across Instagram and Ask.fm to better understand cyberbullying.* Presented at the 2014 IEEE international conference on Big Data and Cloud Computing (BdCloud), pp. 355–362, Sydney, Australia.

Kapidzic, S., & Herring, S. C. (2011). Gender, communication, and self-presentation in teen chatrooms revisited: Have patterns changed? *Journal of Computer-Mediated Communication, 17*(1), 39–59.

Kreager, D. A., & Staff, J. (2009). The sexual double standard and adolescent peer acceptance. *Social Psychology Quarterly, 72*(2), 143–164.

Lenhart, A. (2009). *Teens and sexting how and why minor teens are sending sexually suggestive nude or nearly nude images via text messaging.* Washington, DC: Pew Research Center. (Pew Internet & American Life Project).

Lenhart, A. (2015). *Teens, social media & technology overview 2015.* Retrieved May 3, 2016, from http://www.pewinternet.org/2015/04/09/teens-social-media-technology-2015/

Lippman, J. R., & Campbell, S. W. (2014). Damned if you do, damned if you don't…if you're a girl: Relational and normative contexts of adolescent sexting in the United States. *Journal of Children and Media, 8*(4), 371–386.

Littleton, H. (2011). Rape myths and beyond: A commentary on Edwards and colleagues (2011). *Sex Roles, 65*(11–12), 792–797.

Livingstone, S., & Görzig, A. (2014). When adolescents receive sexual messages on the internet: Explaining experiences of risk and harm. *Computers in Human Behavior, 33*, 8–15.

Mahalik, J. R., Morray, E. B., Coonerty-Femiano, A., Ludlow, L. H., Slattery, S. M., & Smiler, A. (2005). Development of the conformity to feminine norms inventory. *Sex Roles, 52*(7–8), 417–435.

Manago, A. M., Graham, M. B., Greenfield, P. M., & Salimkhan, G. (2008). Self-presentation and gender on MySpace. *Journal of Applied Developmental Psychology, 29*(6), 446–458.

Marks, M. J., & Fraley, R. C. (2005). The sexual double standard: Fact or fiction? *Sex Roles, 52*(3–4), 175–186.

Marwick, A., & boyd, d. (2011). *The drama! Teen conflict, gossip, and bullying in networked publics, SSRN scholarly paper no. ID 1926349.* Rochester, NY: Social Science Research Network.

Mitchell, K., Finkelhor, D., & Wolak, J. (2001). Risk factors for and impact of online sexual solicitation of youth. *JAMA, 285*, 3011–3014. https://doi.org/10.1001/jama.285.23.3011.

Mitchell, K. J., Ybarra, M. L., Jones, L. M., & Espelage, D. (2014). What features make online harassment incidents upsetting to youth? *Journal of School Violence*, 1–23. https://doi.org/10.1080/15388220.2014.990462.

Moore, S., & Rosenthal, D. (2006). *Sexuality in adolescence: Current trends.* Hove, East Sussex: Routledge.

Papp, L. J., Hagerman, C., Gnoleba, M. A., Erchull, M. J., Liss, M., Miles-McLean, H., & Robertson, C. M. (2015). Exploring perceptions of Slut-shaming on Facebook: Evidence for a reverse sexual double standard. *Gender Issues, 32*(1), 57–76.

Poole, E. K. (2014). *Hey girls, did you know? Slut-shaming on the internet needs to stop, SSRN scholarly paper no. ID 2483433.* Rochester, NY: Social Science Research Network.

Rafaeli, S., & Sudweeks, F. (1997). Networked interactivity. *Journal of Computer-Mediated Communication, 2*(4). Available from: http://onlinelibrary.wiley.com/doi/10.1111/j.1083-6101.1997.tb00201.x/full

Ringrose, J. (2011). Are you sexy, flirty, or a slut? Exploring "sexualization"and how teen girls perform/negotiate digital sexual identity on social networking sites. In R. Gill & C. Scharff (Eds.), *New feminities: Postfeminism, neoliberalism and subjectivity* (pp. 99–116). Houndmills/Basingstoke/Hampshire/New York: Palgrave Macmillan.

Ringrose, J., & Barajas, K. (2011). Gendered risks and opportunities? Exploring teen girls' digitised sexual identities in postfeminist media contexts. *International Journal of Media & Cultural Politics, 7*(2), 121–138.

Ringrose, J., Gill, R., Livingstone, S., & Harvey, L. (2012). *A qualitative study of children, young people and "sexting."* A report prepared for the NSPCC.

Ringrose, J., Harvey, L., Gill, R., & Livingstone, S. (2013). Teen girls, sexual double standards and "sexting": Gendered value in digital image exchange. *Feminist Theory, 14*(3), 305–323.

Ringrose, J., & Renold, E. (2010). Normative cruelties and gender deviants: The performative effects of bully discourses for girls and boys in school. *British Educational Research Journal, 36*(4), 573–596.

Robinson, K. (2005). Reinforcing hegemonic masculinities through sexual harassment: Issues of identity, power and popularity in secondary schools. *Gender and Education, 17*(1), 19–37.

Rudman, L. A., Fetterolf, J. C., & Sanchez, D. T. (2013). What motivates the sexual double standard? More support for male versus female control theory. *Personality and Social Psychology Bulletin, 39*(2), 250–263.

Salter, M., Crofts, T., & Lee, M. (2013). *Beyond criminalisation and Responsibilisation: Sexting, gender and young people, SSRN scholarly paper no. ID 2271378.* Rochester, NY: Social Science Research Network.

Skoog, T., & Bayram Özdemir, S. (2016). Physical appearance and sexual activity mediate the link between early puberty and sexual harassment victimization in male adolescents. *Sex Roles, 75*(7–8), 339–348.

Sticca, F., & Perren, S. (2012). Is cyberbullying worse than traditional bullying? Examining the differential roles of medium, publicity, and anonymity for the perceived severity of bullying. *Journal of Youth and Adolescence, 42*(5), 739–750.

Tanenbaum, L. (2015). *I am not a slut.* New York: Harper Collins Publishers.

Walrave, M., & Heirman, W. (2011). Cyberbullying: Predicting victimisation and perpetration. *Children & Society, 25*(1), 59–72.

Walther, J. B., & D'Addario, K. P. (2001). The impacts of emoticons on message interpretation in computer-mediated communication. *Social Science Computer Review, 19*(3), 324–347.

Weiss, K. G. (2010). Too ashamed to report: Deconstructing the shame of sexual victimization. *Feminist Criminology, 5*(3), 286–310.

Ybarra, M. L., Diener-West, M., & Leaf, P. J. (2007). Examining the overlap in internet harassment and school bullying: Implications for school intervention. *Journal of Adolescent Health, 41*(6, Supplement 1), S42–S50.

Ybarra, M. L., & Mitchell, K. (2008). How risky are social networking sites? A comparison of places online where youth sexual solicitation and harassment occurs. *Pediatrics, 121*(2), e350–e357.

CHAPTER 7

A Sexting 'Panic'? What We Learn from Media Coverage of Sexting Incidents

Alyce McGovern and Murray Lee

Abstract This chapter explores media discourses around young people and sexting incidents, with a particular focus on the UK and Australia. Following a review of the literature on media coverage of sexting, the chapter identifies the key themes delineating discussions about young people's sexting. It then moves on to develop an analysis around a number of case studies to demonstrate the ways in which media identifies risks and moral boundaries around people's sexting, and the potential influences of this on public debates around young people's intimate communications. The chapter then reflects on whether these media discourses bear relation to the way in which young people themselves understand sexting behaviours. We conclude by suggesting panic around sexting must be understood in the context of competing discourses around young people and sexual expression.

Keywords Sexting • Media discourses • Sexting epidemic • Gender • Young people

A. McGovern (✉)
School of Social Sciences, UNSW, Sydney, NSW, Australia

M. Lee
Sydney Institute of Criminology, The University of Sydney,
Camperdown, NSW, Australia

© The Author(s) 2018
M. Walrave et al. (eds.), *Sexting*, Palgrave Studies in Cyberpsychology,
https://doi.org/10.1007/978-3-319-71882-8_7

Introduction: Sexting in the Media

In 2013, British soap opera *Hollyoaks* aired a storyline addressing the issue of teen sexting. The plot – which was developed in conjunction with the Child Exploitation and Online Protection centre (CEOP) – involved one of the show's characters, 'Robbie', encouraging his brother 'John' to ask new girlfriend 'Holly' for an image of herself in her underwear. After John receives the image, Robbie gets hold of it and posts it online. Believing the image has been shared online by John, Holly takes revenge by revealing a similar image of John in the window of a local shop (Baxter, 2013). During the airing of these episodes *Hollyoaks* actors also fronted a series of television advertisements from the National Society for the Prevention of Cruelty to Children (NSPCC) alerting young people to the risks of sexting and encouraging girls in particular not to feel pressured to engage in the practice. In 2016, the NSPCC again partnered with a British soap opera, this time *EastEnders,* to provide advice following a storyline in the soap that saw character 'Jay' plead guilty to child pornography charges for videos he possessed of underage character 'Linzi/Star' (Greenwood, 2016; Walker, 2016). The program charted the consequences of Jay's conviction, including being 'ordered to perform 150 hours of community service and sign the sex offenders' register for five years', as well as being kicked out of home (Greenwood, 2016). In a statement directed at parents that was released following the airing of the storyline, the NSPCC said that while 'upsetting' they 'wanted to highlight the pressures facing young people today, particularly around sexting' (EastEnders News Team, 2016). The statement concluded with a lengthy guide for parents on how to talk to their kids about sexting, and what to do if they have been 'affected' by sexting.

These two examples, taken straight from prime-time television screens, are emblematic of a particular level of concern that has increasingly taken hold in the public sphere since the 'arrival' of the teen sexting 'problem'. The discourses such representations offer typically frame sexting as a risky activity, a practice that will cause embarrassment at best, or result in criminal sanctions at worst. Such discourses have permeated media reporting on teen sexting, and arguably have fed into growing concerns about teens involvement in sexting, and the likely implications of that.

It is these and other media discourses that this chapter is interested in exploring. Through an overview of the literature on studies into media coverage of sexting, the chapter identifies some of the key themes delineated in media reporting of young people's sexting. In examining several case studies, primarily from the UK and Australia, that demonstrate the ways in which the media have identified risks and moral boundaries around young people's sexting globally, the chapter considers the potential influences of these sets of discourses on public debates around young people's sexual expression and intimate communications. The chapter concludes by suggesting that while there may indeed be media-driven episodes of panic around sexting, these must be understood in the context of wider competing discourses and experiences of the broad range of behaviours that are encompassed by the notion of sexting, and through the continuity that is the public's moral concern about young people, sexuality and new technologies.

Media Reporting of Sexting: What the Research Tells Us

The term 'sexting' – an amalgamation of the words 'sexy' and 'texting' – is a media created term used primarily by adults to describe a set of practices that have only emerged within the past decade (Albury, Crawford, Byron, & Mathews, 2013; Crofts, Lee, McGovern, & Milivojevic, 2015; Karaian, 2012). While it is acknowledged in the academic literature that the term sexting encompasses a broad spectrum of behaviours and practices (Albury et al., 2013; Crofts et al., 2015), media reports on sexting – particularly as they relate to young people – tend to rely on simplistic or reduced definitions of the practice. As Draper (2012: 222) put it:

> Although the term "sexting" has been used broadly to refer to the transmission of sexually explicit text messages or images using a range of digital technologies, it is also more narrowly constructed as the transmission of nude or semi-nude images or videos using cell phones. (see also Corbett, 2009)

As with other instances where young people, crime, and sexuality intersect, the media have played an important role in shaping public discourse around sexting, framing the act as an issue of concern when practiced by young people (see for example Podlas, 2011). While there have only been a few studies that explicitly examine the ways in which the media have dealt with and responded to young people's sexting (Draper, 2012; Lynn, 2010; Podlas, 2011), these studies have been remarkably consistent in their findings, identifying a set of commonly reproduced media discourses around teen sexting. While there are a number of layers to and interrelationships between these discourses, they can be broken down into four broad themes: prevalence, gender, causes and solutions, and consequences. We will address each in turn.

Prevalence

Studies of media reports of sexting have shown that one dominant discourse – and likely the reason why teen sexting became newsworthy in the first place (Crofts et al., 2015) – is around claims of prevalence, with sexting being framed as a widespread phenomenon (see Crofts et al., 2015; Draper, 2012; Lynn, 2010; Podlas, 2011). These studies highlight that the term 'epidemic' is used with regularity to describe young people's sexting practices, despite the problematic nature of such characterisations. Often such claims are drawn from single reports, or unverified data on the number of cases being dealt with by criminal justice authorities, undercutting more accurate assessments of the complexities underlying young people's involvement in sexting (Crofts et al., 2015). In this way, the message being communicated in the media often exaggerates the real occurrence and frequency of teen sexting, setting up the conditions for a moral panic, whereby societal reaction to teen sexting may arguably be exaggerated and oversimplified (Cohen, 1972).

The 'Epidemic'

The term 'epidemic' is somewhat apt to describe much of the heightened anxiety around sexting given the vague public health discourse around which such stories are often framed. This concern of an 'epidemic' in sexting has shown little evidence of waning in recent years. Indeed, media reports surface regularly – even using the work of the current authors – to identify the scope of the problem. This 2016 *News.com.au* report 'Children as young as 10 years old are sending sexually-explicit images to friends' (Smith, 2016) – with its particular mix of 'expert' opinion, statistics, and moral judgement – is demonstrative of the tenor of this reporting. The article begins by quoting psychologist Michael Carr-Gregg, who expresses concern over young people and their capacity to understand the ramifications of their sexting:

> Mr Carr-Gregg said it was "naive" to think sexting was happening only via text. He said the results are "catastrophic". "Children are getting their

hands on phones from older siblings and being signed up to social media too young by their parents. We're giving them a passport into a very adult world and they don't have the maturity to manage that." (Smith, 2016)

It then moves from discussing the moral concerns of teen sexting to legal considerations:

> ... Legal Aid NSW released a statement in May explaining the risk. "Thousands of children and teenagers are at risk of a criminal record — which can seriously impact their life forever — for sharing nude photos, even if the subject agrees," lawyer Julianne Elliot said. "It is a little known fact that 16-year-olds can legally have sex, but if they take nude photos and share them with one another, they could face serious criminal charges." (Smith, 2016)

Parents too face criticism for their lack of conviction when pressured by their children to allow them access to social media platforms, which are seen to be central to the rise of teen sexting:

> "Parents need to find their digital spine," Mr Carr-Gregg said. "Just because your children are pestering you [to open social media accounts in their name], and because everybody else is on it, doesn't mean you can't stand your ground." (Smith, 2016)

The article concludes by stating that there has been a sharp rise in complaints to the Children's eSafety Commissioner about sexting and intimate images (Smith, 2016). This report highlights well the multiple interlinking discourses around sexting and young people. First, the headline is moralising; hinting that things are getting worse, social standards getting lower. Second, the expert describing the current state of affairs as 'catastrophic' reinforces the moral concerns and the fact that the children involved do not understand the implications of their actions (legally or ethically). These two discourse combine to emphasise the children at risk/ children as a risk dualism which often characterises concerns for young people's welfare – particularly where it concerns sexual or sexualised behaviours. Third is the discourse of parents 'in the dark' – or actively facilitating their child's risky behaviours – needing to develop a 'digital spine'. All this was supported by a simplistic representation of our own data as indicating the high prevalence of sexting (Lee, Crofts, McGovern, & Milivojevic, 2015). However, while indicating that large number of young had tried sexting at least once, our report actually shows that most did not do it often, did it with only one partner, and generally experienced the interactions positively (see Crofts et al., 2015; Lee et al., 2015).

The epidemic discourse is hardly confined to Australian reporting. In the UK *The Independent* reports Britain's schools have been 'hit by sexting epidemic involving children as young as 12' (Fox, 2016), and that '[t]ens of thousands of children have been caught sharing sexual imagery online over the last three years' (Fox, 2016). The situation was reported to be similar in the US with the article 'Sexting 'epidemic' among teens alarms school, law enforcement officials' (Moore, 2016) making headlines in Michigan:

> A girl is ostracized from her athletic team after she sends nude pictures of herself to teammates' boyfriends, as well as other boys at her high school. A videotape of three students engaged in sex inside their high school spreads like wildfire among their classmates. A middle school girl sends nude images of herself to someone she only met online. All these incidents took place in Muskegon County, and are part of what law enforcement officials call "an epidemic" of teen sexting – the transmission of sexual images through such electronic devices as cell phones.

This final iteration of the epidemic, evident in the above quote, also highlights another characteristic of the framing of sexting by young people; its gendered nature.

Gender

Alongside media claims of a teen sexting epidemic sit gendered definitions of the practice. As studies into media reporting of sexting demonstrate, in attempting to make sense of the teen sexting 'epidemic', the media often gender the practice of sexting, with proclamations made that 'girls' are sending sexts to 'boys' as a way of getting their attention (Crofts et al., 2015). By setting up sexting exchanges in this way, the media perpetuate a definition of sexting that positions girls as the duped producers of sexting images, with boys being the wily recipients and, often, the ones who forward such images onto third parties (Crofts et al., 2015; Draper, 2012). Studies have also found that gendered discourses of teen sexting are further reinforced by the ways in which the media articulate the differing consequences for boys and girls who sext (Draper, 2012). For example, for girls, consequences raised often include the potential for emotional distress, the risk of being bullied, and broader reputational harms of participating in sexting (Draper, 2012). On the other hand, for boys consequences are more commonly expressed in legal and economic terms, with their future education and employment prospects of primary concern in media reports (Draper, 2012). Furthermore, the onus of prevention is largely laid on the shoulders of girls, who are expected to guard their sexual purity and desires by abstaining from engaging in sexting (Draper, 2012: 227).

The Gender Myth
On face value, reporting the gendered nature of sexting by young people seems to make complete sense. Young women tend to be more at risk of exploitation, coercion, and pressure to engage in sexting than young men; although as our work and that of others shows, this generalisation is certainly not universal (Crofts et al., 2015; Henry, Powell, & Flynn, 2017; Lee et al., 2015). However, media reporting rarely teases out the reasons for these risks, either placing responsibility for girls' involvement in sexting on their own lack of self-esteem, absence of parental discipline, the increasing pornification of society, or a lack of sexual or technological education (see Crofts et al., 2015). And while at times and for some all these factors may play a part, there are two important silences in much of the reporting. The first is around the need to educate boys about the ethics of online romantic encounters. This silence means that – like early sexual assault prevention discourses and messages – young women are held at least partially responsible for their own victimisation. The second is around desire; that is, young women are constructed as lacking in agency and as being unable to enter into online romantic contexts due to a lack of 'awareness' or their 'compulsive' natures. As a result, they are rendered incapable of managing their romantic or sexualised interactions and constructed as ignorant.

The characterisation of women in this way is apparent in the piece from *The Times*:

> Action needs to be taken by the Scottish government to tackle the problem of "sexting" by teenage girls after figures showed that a worrying number had sent intimate images of themselves on their phones or the internet, watchdogs warned last night. Her Majesty's Inspectorate of Constabulary in Scotland (HMICS) and the Care Inspectorate warn, in a review of the management of sex offenders, that girls are at risk of "exploitation and criminalisation" through sexting. (Gourtsoyannis, 2015)

While not wanting to downplay risks of exploitation for young women, again it is the young women's behaviour that is held to the higher level of scrutiny. These young women are constructed as deceived by a pornified society and online predators, and in need of education about the danger they are putting themselves in.

A recent event in Australia seemed to reinforce these demonstrative risks to young women with little ambiguity. In 2016 *News.com.au* and its affiliates reported: 'Exclusive: Students from 71 Australian schools targeted by sick pornography ring' (Funnell, 2016). The story detailed the practice of 'teen boys and young men secretly swapping and exchanging graphic sexual images of female students and other nonconsenting women' (Funnell, 2016). Reportedly, thousands of images were published on a website housed in the US. Participants in the site could nominate:

> [t]he specific high school or region they are phishing for nude photos from, along with the full names of girls they are "hunting". Hundreds of individual names have appeared on "wanted" lists, including the names of sisters and entire high school friendship circles. (Funnell, 2016)

Excerpts of some of the discussions being conducted on the site were published in the report, including:

> "Anyone have any Wenona wins?"
> "Anyone have any Saint Clare Year 12 wins?"
> "I've got heaps of Miami High girls. Kik me if you wanna trade!"
> "I ripped these from a computer I was asked to fix a few years ago."
> "Who has nudes of this bitch? I hear she throws it around!"
> "I'll [upload] all [the nudes] I have if people start looking for Hunter Valley, Newcastle or Port Macquarie girls, or any hot sluts". (Funnell, 2016)

These highlighted the degrading and yet normalised way the participants discussed their 'trophies', constructing the young women involved as little more than tokens by which the boys could achieve higher status amongst their peers.

Experts appeared out of the woodwork to reinforce that this was 'foreseen' and 'inevitable' and how the boys' behaviour was an expression of the availability of porn on the internet. The episode was unquestionably concerning, however, many details of the case are still to come to light. And while the boys' behaviour was rightly reproached and a criminal investigation undertaken, it was again young women who were held at least partly responsible for their victimisation. As *The Age* newspaper reported, at least one Melbourne school used the 'porn site' incident to attempt to regulate the behaviour of young women at the school:

> Kambrya College, [...] demanded that female students wear skirts that finished below their knees to "protect their integrity". They were also asked on Thursday to stop wearing make-up and sending "sexy selfies". It came a day after the Berwick state school was named on a website run by a global porn ring that posted graphic photos of Australian schoolgirls. The Australian Federal Police said on Friday that authorities had shut the website down. (Cook & Booker, 2016)

Thus, the natural frame of the story was not about the disrespectful and reprehensible behaviour of the boys and men involved (as it had been in Funnell's original story), but how young girls needed to regulate their own behaviour such that the almost 'naturalised' actions of the boys would be more difficult to undertake. Girls were essentially meant to 'target harden' themselves – to draw on the language of situational crime prevention literature.

And while some of the subsequent reportage on the issue was more measured and rational, there was also confusion about the framing. This confusion was often the result of the competing discourses of experts and the variety of moral entrepreneurs involved in sexting debates. This was demonstrated by a later article published in *The Courier Mail*. This excerpt from the article begins with a quote from a Queensland police officer working on the case, but the paper then links the story about the site unproblematically with statistical data and anecdotal evidence on sexual assault as if this link is self-evident:

> "The sort of porn we're seeing now is markedly different to 10, even five years ago," he says. "It's brutalizing, or humiliating, or degrading, and it drums home the lie, again and again, that this is what girls want." Rouse shakes his head. "I think we're going to see some pretty alarming consequences from all of this."

> The most recent Australian Bureau of Statistics figures suggest we already may be, with 2003 youths making up 27 per cent of sexual assault perpetrators in Australia in 2015 – 770 of them aged between 10 and 14. Earlier this year, at a Brisbane primary school, a six-year-old boy was repeatedly molested in the school toilets by two older boys; last month in NSW, two 12-year-old

boys in Year 6 at a northern beaches public school were charged over alleg-
edly raping a six-year-old Year 1 student in the school's toilet block; and in
Caboolture, north of Brisbane, police are investigating a case of sexual
assault by a nine-year-old boy on a four-year-old girl. (Whiting, 2016)

Quite apart from the framing of these reports is the problem that media
reporting on young people sexting thrives on stories of sexual exploitation
and sexting gone wrong. Yet, as the current authors (Crofts et al., 2015;
Lee et al., 2015) and others (Englander, 2012) have continually argued,
based on strong empirical evidence, most sexting by young people does
not go wrong. Few participants report being exploited through consensual activity, and of those that do feel pressured the majority report no
explicit negative outcomes once they send an image (Englander, 2012).
While that certainly does not justify the coercion or pressure, it does indicate we have to be careful applying a one size fits all model to its
outcomes.

This is not to suggest there are no dangers involved with young people
sexting: clearly there are (cf. Henry et al., 2017). However, media reportage often overstates these, misrepresents the problem, and largely fails to
report what young people themselves constantly report when given a
voice; that sexting can be pleasurable, if slightly risky, fun.

Causes and Solutions

In analysing the teen sexting 'epidemic', it is not uncommon for media and
commentators to attempt to attribute blame for young people's involvement
in sexting and, similarly, look for solutions to the 'problem'. Such attempts
often result in the media painting a somewhat grim picture of the capacity of
teens as decision makers and parents and teachers as (moral) guardians. For
example, both Draper (2012) and Podlas (2011) found that the media often
depict young people as being unable to understand the consequences of
their behaviour. Such discourses were also identified by Lynn (2010) and
Crofts et al. (2015), who found that the media tend to correlate biological
determinism with young people's decision making around sexting; that is,
the media attribute young people's decision to sext as being due to their
brain development, or lack thereof. Lynn (2010) further found that biological discourses – which focused on the moral and intellectual development of
contemporary teens – were often used in conjunction with social factors,
such as peer pressure or lascivious media content, to undermine the capacity

of teens to understand or control their own actions. In this way, studies into media reports of teen sexting have found that the narrative often painted by the press is that of 'impulsive', 'libidinous' teens, 'lacking self-control' (Lynn, 2010: 1; Podlas, 2011).

Along with explanations that seek to understand why young people might choose to sext, media discourses also interrogate the role of technological advancements in contributing to the practice. For example, studies from Draper (2012: 225) and Lynn (2010: 4) found that technological determinism was often cited as a causal factor in sexting, driving or 'seducing' young people – especially girls – to engage in sexting. According to their findings, the message being communicated in the media is that young people cannot be trusted to use technology responsibly.

Beyond teens themselves, however, parents also come under scrutiny from the media with regards to their relationship with, and understanding of, technology. Specifically, as a number of studies have found, media discourses tend to characterise parents as 'clueless' and 'inept' when it comes to technology (Crofts et al., 2015; Draper, 2012: 226, 229; Lynn, 2010: 11), and therefore unable to understand their own children's engagement with technology, further contributing to the 'problem' of sexting.

When it comes to the media offering solutions to the teen sexting 'epidemic', institutional and individual surveillance (Crofts et al., 2015; Draper, 2012; Lynn, 2010) are commonly called upon as effective mechanisms through which to prevent or intervene in young people's sexting (Taylor, 2013). It is clear in such media discourses that parents and educators are framed as bearing the responsibility for deterring young people from engaging in sexting. For parents advice is articulated in a range of ways, from providing appropriate 'moral guidance' to teens, through to using surveillance techniques – such as monitoring their teen's digital devices manually or through tracking technology – to ensure the safety of their children. Parents are further encouraged to limit the access their children have to technology if surveillance strategies are not successful and seek training to better understand their children's online activities. In many respects, technology is positioned as both the cause of and solution to teen sexting.

Discourses of surveillance are not just aimed at parents, however. Educators are also encouraged to use surveillance due to their role as guardians of teens' safety (Draper, 2012; Lynn, 2010). The responsibility for implementing educative approaches more broadly is also laid at the feet of adults, who are encouraged to school teens on the dangers of sexting as the best approach to discourage it (Draper, 2012: 230). Such discourses tend to take a risk-centric approach and encourage adults to educate young people about the potential ramifications of sexting (Crofts et al., 2015). Parents are encouraged to speak with their teens (Lynn, 2010: 12–13) and frame sexting in terms of severe disciplinary consequences, taking a "zero tolerance" approach that posits a message of abstinence as being the only way to secure against the risks of sexting.

The Problem of Technology

In each generation, it seems, technological developments are perceived as cause for alarm; from the telephone, to television and the internet, advancements in communications technologies bring with them a raft of concerns about their impact on society and, in particular, young people. When it comes to sexting – a practice that is linked with mobile and internet technologies – this seems especially true. The article 'Sext addicts: How British parents are paying £70,000 to send their teenagers on specialist therapy courses abroad to stop them sending naked photos' (Hind, 2017) published in the UK newspaper, *The Daily Mail*, encapsulates many of the most sensationalist problem/solution discourses when it comes to teen sexting and technology. The article begins by outlining the increasing number of teens being put through specialist therapy by their parents because of their sexting 'addiction':

> The Mail on Sunday has established that increasing numbers of desperate British parents are spending £70,000 a time on specialist courses of therapy abroad at centres like these, because their daughters have become hopelessly hooked on sending naked photographs of themselves using their mobile phones and the internet.

> Specialists here at the Yes We Can Youth Clinic in Holland say that the facility is inundated with enquires from British families, and that dozens of British girls have already been booked in for addiction to sexting after suffering catastrophic mental breakdowns, including depression and suicidal feelings. (Hind, 2017)

Here we see these narratives of technological determinism evident in the representation of young women as 'hopelessly hooked' to sexting, seemingly unable to extract themselves from the lure of technology without some form of external, adult intervention. There is also a healthy dose of biological determinism thrown for good measure; in this case, it is specialist clinics who come to the rescue, sought out by parents seeking solutions to their teens' 'problem'.

The same article goes on to document the dangers of ignoring the 'problem', first by likening this addition gambling or drug addiction:

> To many teenagers, sexting it is just a high-tech way of fooling around.
>
> Yet the founder of the clinic, Jan Willem Poot, said it can have the same destructive effects as drugs or gambling on its victims – predominantly girls – who grow ever more hungry for the excitement and attention of exposing themselves online.
>
> In fact, it is the fastest-growing addiction among young women, matched only by addiction to computer games among young men. (Hind, 2017)

Again, here we see the different ways in which the 'problem' is characterised for males and females, with female addiction to sexting being contrasted with males' presumably worrisome, but overall less concerning, addiction to gaming.

The long-term impacts of this 'addiction' are also considered, including the suggestion that in searching for the supposed 'high' sexting brings, teen girls might even turn to sex work:

> Mr Poot is particularly concerned that the consequences are long-term and can lead girls to indulge in serious risk-taking behaviour – and even prostitution – as the addiction takes hold, in the search for a similar but ever-more intense 'high'.
>
> [...]
>
> 'Sexting has become such a big problem and we are treating many girls for it, now from Britain as well. It is attention-seeking at its most extreme...' (Hind, 2017)

The solution floated is thus intensive therapy:

> Psychotherapists say that sending of a 'sext' message can produce an addictive rush of chemicals, similar to the effect of taking drugs. And according to Mr Poot, these consequences can be so serious that they cannot be resolved within once-a-week standard therapy sessions.

> 'At this point something more intensive needs to be done or their behaviour is at risk of getting worse,' he said. 'It starts around the age of 13 and if it isn't treated, it gets worse and some of them will end up offering or selling their bodies to get that same feeling – that "wow" feeling.' (Hind, 2017)

As well as attributing blame to 'extreme attention-seeking behaviour' from 'girls', experts are also cited to reinforce the scientific features of addiction in these cases, addictions so serious that they require more than 'standard' solutions. Reflecting discourses that encourage parents to seek out additional assistance should they be unable to deal with the 'problem', the article goes on to spell out the risks of failing to act, including the claim that girls may 'indulge in serious risk-taking behaviour – and even prostitution' if left untreated (Hind, 2017).

Such characterisations undoubtedly have the capacity to contribute to panics about the effects of technology and are reflected in political stances that attempt to regulate technology as a way of stopping the problem altogether. UK Secretary of State for Health Jeremy Hunt, for example, as cited in *The Guardian* (Press Association, 2016), called for a 'crackdown' on the technology industry, stating:

> Under-18s should be prevented by social media companies from texting sexually explicit images, the health secretary has said...
> [...]
> "For example, I just ask myself the simple question as to why it is that you can't prevent the texting of sexually explicit images by people under the age of 18, if that's a lock that parents choose to put on a mobile phone contract. Because there is technology that can identify sexually explicit pictures and prevent it being transmitted".

Such solutions are representative of discourses identified in the literature that cite institutional surveillance as an effective strategy to prevent or intervene in young people's sexting activities, yet fail to engage with the range of ethics-based educative models that might equally offer something in relation to the issues raised.

Consequences

As has already been indicated, academic studies into media discourses of teen sexting have shown the tendency for the media to focus on the likely and possible consequences for teens that engage in the practice. These consequences not only exist on a spectrum, from embarrassment through to criminal charges, but are also heavily gendered, as noted above. Studies have shown that personal and social harms form a key part of the discourses disseminated in media reports of the consequences of teen sexting.

These harms are typically communicated in terms of character-related concerns, such as the threat or damage to a youth's reputation or the potential for embarrassment or shaming. Such themes have been highlighted by Draper (2012: 226; see also Albury et al., 2013; Gabriel, 2014), who found that even within these frames, character risks were more likely to be raised in relation to girls than boys. For boys, rather than focusing on character, media reports tend to examine the future prospects of the individual. So, for example, official or legal action taken as a result of their involvement in sexting is seen to potentially threaten a boy's future education, career and employment prospects (Crofts et al., 2015; Draper, 2012: 227). As such, much like attempts to define or apportion blame for sexting, gender similarly plays a significant role in media attempts to indicate ramifications.

Beyond reputational concerns, the permanency of sexting images is also a theme that is often raised in media reports. In particular, it is not uncommon for such discourses to raise the possibility of such images ending up in the hands of paedophiles (Crofts et al., 2015; Podlas, 2011), tapping into broader societal fears about the 'shadowy figure' of the paedophile, a reductive frame that underplays the fact that sexual violence is more likely to occur in the home (Kitzinger, 2002). At the more extreme end of the spectrum Podlas (2011: 33–34), for example, found that media coverage of teen suicides in the wake of sexting-related incidents were often used by the media as 'cautionary tales' about the potential risks of sexting to teens.

Alongside the themes of social and personal risks and harms for teens who sext sit discourses on the potential legal consequences for young people who send and receive sexts (Crofts et al., 2015; Lynn, 2010; Podlas, 2011). In particular, it is the risk of being charged with child pornography offences that permeates media reports across jurisdictions. Being added to a sex offender register is one of the primary risks raised in media reports about the legal consequences of sexting (Crofts et al., 2015). These discourses are often reinforced by media reports that cite primary definers, or experts – such as the police or other criminal justice officials – who are regularly called upon to reinforce the 'illegality' of the practice for those underage (and therefore its potentially criminal consequences) or, somewhat less frequently, on the possibility of diversion (Crofts et al., 2015; Lynn, 2010).

Interestingly, while media discourses tend to focus on the criminal consequences of sexting, there is evidence of an emerging set of media discourse that present a more critical picture of legal interventions, with studies finding that some media reports tend to reflect critically on official legal intervention in teen sexting, instead canvassing a range of potential legal reforms that might better respond to teen sexting. Such reports often question the appropriateness of the sex offenders register as a response to teen sexting (Crofts et al., 2015). For example, moves by police to 'formally adopt a policy emphasising education over punishment' in response to rising rates of sexting amongst teens, have been praised by experts and are indicative of a growing level of nuance in media reports on the teen sexting phenomenon (Hunt, 2017).

Criminalising Sexting

When reports surfaced in May 2017 that nearly 1,500 children had been convicted for child exploitation material in the Australian state of Queensland (Hunt, 2017), the media response was one of surprise. While over the years many had speculated about the potentially criminal consequences of teen sexting (see Crofts et al., 2015 for a discussion on this), and indeed many a think piece had been written on what to make of the teen sexting phenomenon, these reports were the first that seemingly confirmed that large numbers of young people were coming to the attention of law enforcement officials for sexting-based offences. As Hunt describes in her article 'Sexting to blame for nearly 1,500 children convicted for child exploitation':

> Of the 3,035 offenders dealt with by the criminal justice system in Queensland for child exploitation material in the 10 years to 30 June 2016, 1,498 were under 17, initial analysis of the data has found.

> Twenty-eight were sentenced in court. Of the remaining 1,470 to receive diversion, the vast majority received a formal caution from police (92.9%), with 7.1% referred to the restorative justice process and required to attend a youth conference.

> Most of the diverted young offenders were engaged in "sexting-based offences", with about an even split between possession (35.4%), distribution (34.4%) and production (29.7%).

Beyond simply focusing on the raw figures, however, the article also engaged with measures being adopted to try and divert young people from criminal justice responses to sexting. For example, the article goes on to explain that the increase in young people engaging in sexting had prompted police to consider an educative approach to dealing with the issue:

> Direction for officers responding to "circumstances involving young people of similar age sexting or engaging in consenting sexual experimentation" was incorporated into the [Queensland Police Service] Operational Procedures Manual in November 2016, with the guidance that the focus should be on prevention and education.
>
> Grounds for a criminal investigation would be established by taking into account factors including whether the person was consenting, the context in which the sharing occurred, the age of the involved parties and the relationship (Hunt, 2017).

While still taking a punitive approach, there are similar signs in other jurisdictions that a more muted criminal justice response is being considered for teens, particularly when engaging in consensual sexting. For example, *The Denver Post* (Paul, 2017) reported in 2017 that Colorado Governor John Hickenlooper was expected to sign off on a 'compromise' bill that would:

> make consensual exchanges of nude images by children a civil infraction [rather than a felony offence] and gives prosecutors a range of options — from a petty offense to a felony — to use against teens who possess or distribute sexts against a victim's will.

Such moves mirror more recent studies and reports that increasingly distinguish between consensual teen sexting and image based abuse (see Henry et al., 2017).

Conclusion

This chapter has sought to demonstrate key media and popular discourses in regard to the practice of young people engaging in sexting. In drawing on illustrative media case studies we have shown that understandings of the prevalence, gendered double standards, causes, and solutions around young people and sexting have all been subject to moralising and pathologising in media representations. Such representations reduce our ability develop reasoned and empirically based solutions to the education and harm reduction approaches which should be deployed such that young people clearly understand the implications of their intimate online interactions.

However, while the bulk of media discussion about teen sexting has been sensationalist and dramatic in nature, there are signs that more recent coverage of the issues has been more nuanced, at least in their reflections on criminal justice responses. Recent media reports have tended to identify some of the problems that existing legal frameworks create when applied to teen sexting, and alternative approaches have been considered both in public and political responses to the issue. There is still some way to go, however, in challenging the gendered nature of reporting on sexting and presenting the broader range of behaviours and experiences for teens who engage in sexting. To do this, the media will need to move beyond simplistic definitions and cautionary tales that establish moralising narratives for the experiences of boys and girls who engage in sexting. Future research may also consider the range of ways in which teen sexting is approached in media reports from different cultural and geographical locales.

REFERENCES

Albury, K., Crawford, K., Byron, P., & Mathews, B. (2013). *Young people and sexting in Australia: Ethics, representation and the law.* ARC Centre for Creative Industries and Innovation/Journalism and Media Research Centre, The University of New South Wales, Australia. Available at http://www.cci.edu.au/sites/default/files/Young_People_And_Sexting_Final.pdf

Baxter, H. (2013, November 19). Hollyoaks sexting storyline highlights dangers for teenagers. *The Guardian.* Retrieved September 8, 2016 https://www.theguardian.com/lifeandstyle/2013/nov/18/hollyoaks-sexting-storyline-dangers-teenagers-nspcc

Cohen, S. (1972). *Moral panics and folk devils.* London: MacGibbon & Kee.

Cook, H., & Booker, C. (2016, August 19). No short skirts, no make-up, no 'sexy selfies' – School accused of 'slut-shaming'. *The Age.* Retrieved December 10, 2016 http://www.theage.com.au/victoria/no-short-skirts-no-makeup-no-sexy-selfies--school-accused-of-slutshaming-20160819-gqwq6m.html

Corbett, D. (2009). Let's talk about sext: The challenge of funding the right legal response to the teenage practice of "sexting". *Journal of Internet Law, 13*(6), 3–8.

Crofts, T., Lee, M., McGovern, A., & Milivojevic, S. (2015). *Sexting and young people.* London: Palgrave Macmillan.

Draper, N. (2012). Is your teen at risk? Discourses of adolescent sexting in United States television news. *Journal of Children and Media, 6*(2), 221–236.

EastEnders News Team. (2016, April 27). Jay's story: NSPCC advice on sexting. *BBC One EastEnders Blog.* Retrieved September 8, 2016 http://www.bbc. co.uk/blogs/eastenders/entries/4ecd37fa-fb41-4d7b-9ec6-ad1aa8b46e9b

Englander, E. (2012). Low risk associated with most teenage sexting: A study of 617 18-year-olds. *MARC Research Report.* Retrieved May 20, 2017 http:// vc.bridgew.edu/cgi/viewcontent.cgi?article=1003&context=marc_reports

Fox, T. (2016, March 12). Britain's schools 'hit by sexting epidemic involving children as young as 12'. *The Independent.* Retrieved April 21, 2017 http:// www.independent.co.uk/news/education/education-news/sexting-britains-school-children-hit-by-epidemic-a6927041.html

Funnell, N. (2016, August 17). Exclusive: Students from 71 Australian schools targeted by sick pornography ring. *News.com.au.* Retrieved April 21, 2017 http://www.news.com.au/lifestyle/real-life/news-life/students-from-70-australian-schools-targeted-by-sick-pornography-ring/news-story/532885 36e0ce3bba7955e92c7f7fa8da.

Gabriel, F. (2014). Sexting, selfies and self-harm: Young people, social media and the performance of self-development. *Media International Australia, 151,* 104–112.

Gourtsoyannis, P. (2015, November 27). Alarm at rise in sexting by teenage girls. *The Times.* Retrieved April 21, 2017 https://www.thetimes.co.uk/article/ alarm-at-rise-in-sexting-by-teenage-girls-qr0t2l2cq5s

Greenwood, C. (2016, April 27). EastEnders Jay Brown Pleads GUILTY to child porn charges before being beaten to a Pulp by Linzi's brothers. *Mirror.* Retrieved September 8, 2016 http://www.mirror.co.uk/tv/tv-news/ eastenders-jay-brown-pleads-guilty-7847001

Henry, N., Powell, A., & Flynn, A. (2017). *Not just 'revenge pornography': Australians' experiences of image based abuse: A summary report.* Melbourne, Australia: RMIT University.

Hind, K. (2017, April 2). Sext addicts: How British parents are paying £70,000 to send their teenagers on specialist therapy courses abroad to stop them sending naked photos. *Daily Mail.* Retrieved May 12, 2017 http://www.dailymail. co.uk/news/article-4371936/Parents-pay-70k-send-teens-course-stop-sexting.html#ixzz4gpkL33Pc

Hunt, E. (2017, May 9). Sexting to blame for nearly 1,500 children convicted for child exploitation. *The Guardian.* Retrieved May 12, 2017 https://www.the-guardian.com/australia-news/2017/may/09/sexting-guidelines-created-by-queensland-police-as-child-convictions-soar

Karaian, L. (2012). Lolita speaks: "Sexting", teenage girls and the law. *Crime Media Culture, 8*(1), 57–73.

Kitzinger, J. (2002). The ultimate neighbour from hell? Stranger danger and the media framing of paedophiles. In Y. Jewkes & G. Letherby (Eds.), *Criminology: A reader.* London: Sage.

Lee, M., Crofts, T., McGovern, A., & Milivojevic, S. (2015). *Sexting and young people: Report to criminology research council.* Canberra: Australian Institute of Criminology. http://www.criminologyresearchcouncil.gov.au/reports/1516/53-1112-FinalReport.pdf

Lynn, R. (2010). *Constructing parenthood in moral panics of youth, digital media and sexting.* 105th annual meeting of the American Sociological Association, Atlanta, GA, 14–17 August.

Moore, L. (2016, June 30). Sexting 'epidemic' among teens alarms school, law enforcement officials. *Michigan Live.* Retrieved April 21, 2017 http://www.mlive.com/news/muskegon/index.ssf/2016/06/sexting_epidemic_among_teens_a.html

Paul, J. (2017, May 6). After two years of debate, Colorado teen sexting bill heads to Gov. John Hickenlooper. *The Denver Post.* Retrieved May 20, 2017 http://www.denverpost.com/2017/05/06/teen-sexting-bill-john-hickenlooper/

Podlas, K. (2011). The "legal epidemiology" of the teen sexting epidemic: How the media influenced a legislative outbreak. *Pittsburgh Journal of Technology Law and Policy, 12,* 1–48.

Press Association. (2016, November 30). Jeremy Hunt proposes Ban on sexting for under-18s. *The Guardian.* Retrieved April 20, 2017 https://www.theguardian.com/society/2016/nov/29/jeremy-hunt-proposes-ban-on-sexting-for-under-18s

Smith, R. (2016, September 26). Children as young as 10 years old are sending sexually-explicit images to friends. *News.com.au.* Retrieved April 20, 2017 http://www.news.com.au/lifestyle/parenting/children-as-young-as-10-years-old-are-sending-sexuallyexplicit-images-to-friends/news-story/6723b343c7566ae77a060425543c49d7

Taylor, E. (2013). *Surveillance schools: Security, discipline and control in contemporary education.* London: Palgrave Macmillan.

Walker, D. (2016, April 28). EastEnders and NSPCC issue sexting words of warning following Jay and Linzi's shock storyline. *Mirror.* Retrieved September 8, 2016 http://www.mirror.co.uk/tv/tv-news/eastenders-nspcc-issue-sexting-words-7854745

Whiting, F. (2016, October 8). Sexting: Should teens be left to their own devices? *The Courier Mail.* Retrieved April 20, 2017 http://www.couriermail.com.au/news/queensland/sexting-should-teens-be-left-to-their-own-devices/news-story/06e70444541903a04965f71a53c7aa0b

CHAPTER 8

Sexting and the Law

Thomas Crofts and Eva Lievens

Abstract This chapter explores the laws that frame sexting with a particular focus on Australia and Europe. International concerns over the impact that new technologies have had on child pornography and child abuse have led to countries strengthening laws to protect children. The chapter analyses how such reforms have impacted on children who engage in sexting and whether children have been criminalised for sexting behaviours. It will be seen that there are differences in how countries approach sexting. This chapter concludes by assessing whether, and what form of, legal response to sexting is appropriate and necessary.

Keywords Sexting • children's rights • Legislation • Non-consensual dissemination of sexual images • Privacy • Non-legal responses

T. Crofts (✉)
Sydney Institute of Criminology, The University of Sydney,
Camperdown, NSW, Australia

E. Lievens
Faculty of Law, Human Rights Centre, Ghent University, Ghent, Belgium

© The Author(s) 2018   119
M. Walrave et al. (eds.), *Sexting*, Palgrave Studies in Cyberpsychology,
https://doi.org/10.1007/978-3-319-71882-8_8

INTRODUCTION

Digital technologies have become central to young people's lives and are 'a vital part of their social life and the building of their identity' (McGrath, 2009, p. 2). A significant factor in young people's socialization, sexual exploration and use of new technologies has been the phenomenon termed 'sexting'.[1] While the term sexting was originally used to denote the sending or receiving of sexually explicit text messages (Rosenberg, 2011) it is now more commonly associated with the digital taking and sharing of intimate (nude, semi-nude, sexualized) images[2] through mobile phone apps or social networking sites. As the Law Reform Committee of Victoria (VLRC) notes, the term 'sexting' is, however, not static but rather, evolving and 'encompasses a wide range of practices, motivations and behaviours' (2013, p. 15). Examples given by the VLRC include images consensually taken and consensually shared with friends for fun or with a boyfriend or girlfriend or potential boyfriend or girlfriend in order to flirt. However, images may also be shared non-consensually for various reasons, including cyberbullying or getting revenge on an ex-partner. Further scenarios include images taken and shared non-consensually, such as up-skirting or images of a sexual assault (VLRC, 2013).[3]

Unsurprisingly the question of how, and whether, the law should be used to respond to these varied forms of behaviour is a vexed and controversial issue and the subject of much debate in legal, political and social discourse (Crofts et al., 2015; Lievens, 2014). Some do not view sexting by children as a significantly new phenomenon rather they see it as children exploring their sexuality as they have always done, albeit with the use of new technologies (Bond, 2011; Cumming, 2009). According to such views it is merely the form of the flirtatious note that has changed to become more technological (Ostrager, 2010) or a change in the location in which such explorations take place, shifting from 'real space', such as behind the bike-shed, to the 'virtual space' (Bond, 2011). However, others argue, for instance 'that devices such as smartphones and practices such as sexting have come to stand for a society losing control over the actions of young people and the morals by which they live their sexual lives' (De Ridder, 2017). Views on what should be done about sexting by children range from insistence that sexting should be considered a form of child pornography and children should be prosecuted under such laws to the stance that children should be protected from such harsh and inappropriate laws. There are also arguments that new offences need to be created to capture the wrong at the core of sexting: the non-consensual distribution of intimate images, and not just for cases of children but also adults (see for instance Commonwealth of Australia, 2016; Beyens & Lievens, 2016). Another approach is to see education about cyber-safety, either alongside criminal law responses or as an alternative to such approaches, as the key to addressing sexting (see for instance VLRC, 2013).

Such divergent views have led to differences in how countries have approached the phenomenon of children engaging in sexting. This chapter will explore the legal responses in the Australian jurisdictions and in Europe.[4] It will show why there has been such a strong focus on the appropriateness of applying child pornography laws to sexting in some jurisdictions. It will do this by first examining the international context to child pornography laws and then in turn exploring the legal responses in the Australian jurisdictions and in Europe. The chapter will close with an assessment of whether, and what form of, legal response is appropriate and necessary to sexting.

INTERNATIONAL FRAMEWORK

Gillespie (2010, p. 19) notes that the concept of combatting child pornography as a harm distinct from other forms of obscene material began to develop around the 1970s. Such concern was picked up by the international community with the recognition that effective laws and greater international cooperation are necessary to combat child pornography. This is reflected for instance in the United Nations *Convention on the Rights of the Child* (UNCRC), which in art 34 requires that:

> States Parties undertake to protect the child from all forms of sexual exploitation and sexual abuse. For these purposes, States Parties shall in particular take all appropriate national, bilateral and multilateral measures to prevent … [t]he exploitative use of children in pornographic performances and materials.

In more recent years recognition of the impact that new technologies have had on the creation, possession and distribution of child pornography alongside greater understanding of the harms associated with child pornography and what should be considered as child pornography has led to broad international agreement about the need to strengthen child pornography laws. In 1996 at the First World Congress Against the Sexual Exploitation of Children a Declaration and Agenda for Action called on States to: 'Criminalize the commercial sexual exploitation of children, as well as other forms of sexual exploitation' and 'Review and revise, where appropriate, laws, policies, programmes and practices to eliminate the commercial sexual exploitation of children'. Soon after the UN adopted an *Optional Protocol on the Sale of Children, Child Prostitution and Child Pornography* in 2000, which entered into force in 2002. In line with mounting concern 'about the growing availability of child pornography on the Internet and other evolving technologies' the Protocol contained a number of recommendations for law reform. Many countries have now adopted these recommendations and changed their laws in relation to child pornography.

The Protocol particularly calls for an expanded definition of what amounts to child pornography. The Optional Protocol defines 'child pornography' to include 'any representation ... of a child engaged in real or simulated sexual activities or any representation of the sexual parts of a child for primarily sexual purposes' (art 2(c)). This broad definition of child pornography accords with the recognition that it is not just images of children directly involved in sexual activity that are of interest to adults with a sexual interest in children. Some images, such as family snaps of a naked child in the bath or at the beach, might be relatively innocent in a general context but they may be sexualised by the viewer (see Taylor & Quayle, 2003, p. 193). Research into online possession of child abuse material shows that there is:

> enormous variety in the types of images collected by adults with a sexual interest in children. While there is almost universal condemnation of the sexual exploitation of children through such images, it is not possible to define precisely what constitutes an illegal child sexual abuse image. This is because the concept is broad, changeable and, at the margins, elusive (Makkai, 2005, p. 1).

The Combatting Paedophile Information Networks in Europe (COPINE) Project has developed a typology of material that might be sexualised by an adult on a 10-point scale, which ranges from sadistic/bestiality at one extreme to indicative non-erotic or sexualised images at the other (see Taylor, Holland, & Quayle, 2001, p. 101). Interestingly, the Protocol does not define the age at which a person should be considered a child for the purposes of child pornography laws, however, the UNCRC defines 'a child' as every human being below the age of eighteen years unless under the law applicable to the child majority is attained earlier. Along the same lines the Council of Europe Convention on Cybercrime (2001) sets the age at 18 (but does allow a State to have a lower age level, but not lower than 16 (art 9(3)). Many jurisdictions have amended child pornography laws to be consistent with these international obligations.

It is particularly these two developments, the setting of the age of 18 as demarking a child for the purposes of child pornography laws and the relatively broad definition of child pornography that mean that children can be prosecuted under child pornography laws for sexting. It appears that there was little consideration given in debates about strengthening laws to protect children about the possibility that the laws may be used against children. The following will trace how such laws have been implemented and the debate about the appropriateness of applying such laws to children.

AUSTRALIAN LAWS

Child Pornography Laws

Australia has a system of federal (Commonwealth) and State/Territory criminal law. In line with its international obligations relating to combatting child pornography the Commonwealth Government has taken 'an important leadership role in this area' by creating new Commonwealth offences and definitions designed to 'provide a springboard to a national approach to this issue' (Slipper, 2004, pp. 32035–32036). Child pornography is defined in s 473.1 of the Commonwealth Criminal Code Act 1995 as material that depicts or describes a person (or a representation of a person) who is under 18 years old (or who appears to be under 18), either engaged in (or appearing to be engaged in), a sexual pose or sexual activity or in the presence of a person who is engaged in (or appears to be engaged in) a sexual pose or sexual activity. The definition also includes material where the dominant characteristic of that material is the depiction, description or representation for a sexual purpose, of the sexual organ, anal region or breasts (of a female person), who is, or who appears to be under 18. In all these instances the depiction or description must be framed in such a way that reasonable persons would regard as being, in all the circumstances, offensive. This latter provision is designed to prevent overreach of the law and ensure that community standards are incorporated into the determination of whether the material should amount to child pornography (Krone, 2005, p. 2). Commonwealth offences include using a carriage service (e.g., telephone, mobile telephone, internet etc.) to access, transmit or make child pornography available (Criminal Code Act 1995 (Cth), s 474.19). It is also an offence to possess or produce child pornography with the intent to place it on the internet (Criminal Code Act 1995 (Cth), ss 474.20, 474.23). The States and Territories all have laws prohibiting child pornography, some jurisdictions more closely following the Commonwealth jurisdiction than others (see Crofts & Lee, 2013).

In Australia debate has shifted from calls for the law to respond to sexting by children to expressions of concern that prosecuting children under child pornography laws is too severe a reaction (see Crofts et al., 2015). It is, however, hard to gain a clear picture of whether children are being prosecuted under child pornography laws in large numbers. Despite some early media claims that many children were being prosecuted other reports suggest that the number of prosecutions are low and that children are mainly diverted from prosecution by police. The latter view is supported by comments by the Acting Commander of Victoria Police who, while giving evidence before the Victorian Law Reform Committee Inquiry into Sexting, noted that no one under 18 years of age had been prosecuted under child pornography laws in Victoria for sexting alone (Paterson, 2012, p. 13). It seems then that children in Australia are not being routinely prosecuted under child pornography laws (see Crofts et al., 2015).

Nonetheless, there seems to be little appetite to completely remove children from the reaches of child pornography laws. In 2010 there was debate in the Australian Parliament about the issue of children being prosecuted under child pornography offences for 'sexting' and whether some exception should apply. Brendan O'Connor, Minister for Home Affairs, was not in favour of a blanket ban on the prosecution of children for 'sexting' or the creation of a defence on the basis that:

> Excluding the sending of child pornography or child abuse material by young people from the proposed offences would be inappropriate, as it might reduce protections for young people. For example, instances of young people sending sexually explicit images of themselves or other young people

may in some cases be malicious or exploitative. Although the child pornography offences could potentially apply to young people, there is scope for law enforcement and prosecution agencies to take the circumstances of a particular case into account before proceeding to investigate or proceeding to prosecute. (O'Connor, 2010, p. 2052)

Following this debate rather than exclude children from the reach of child pornography offences the Criminal Code Act 1995 (Cth) was amended so that the permission of the Attorney-General is required before a child under 18 can be prosecuted under child pornography laws (ss273.2A and 474.24C, inserted by Crimes Legislation Amendment (Sexual Offences Against Children) Bill 2010).

The only jurisdiction in Australia to conduct a review of the laws relating to sexting so far has been Victoria. The Victorian Law Reform Committee also did not recommend removing children completely from the reaches of child pornography laws but did recommend the extension of defences to all child pornography offences for children[5] alongside the creation of new sexting specific offences (discussed below) and the development of holistic cyber safety education programmes focussed on 'developing positive practices for engagement with the online world' (VLRC, 2013, p. 53). Developing defences to child pornography offences is appropriate because when young people create, possess or send nude and semi-nude images in the main they are doing so for reasons quite different to an adult who has a sexual interest in children. Several studies have shown that largely children send sexts for fun or to be flirty as part of normal sexual development and they generally do not distribute such images widely (Crofts et al., 2015; see also Lee & Crofts, 2015 for a summary of recent research). Sexts are generally not used for exploitative reasons or to cause harm to the subject of the image (this does not mean that they may nonetheless cause harm or that there are cases where there is an intention to exploit or harm). Furthermore, sexting generally does not indicate a problematic expression of sexuality. As the VLRC notes:

> their motivation is to obtain explicit images of people in their age group, at a similar stage of physiological and psychological development, and with similar interests. In the vast majority of cases, as these children grow older, their sexual interests will remain with their peers ... [they] are not paedophiles in the making, but instead are experiencing a phase of normal development. (VLRC, 2013, p. 139)

Sexting Specific Offence

The VLRC felt that generally children should not be prosecuted under child pornography laws even where the image was distributed non-consensually, rather the Committee recommended that there was a need for a new offence to cover such situations. Following this recommendation the Victorian parliament enacted two new offences covering the distribution of an intimate image and the threat to distribute an intimate image (ss 41DA and 41DB Summary Offences Act 1966 (Vic) inserted by Crimes Amendment (Sexual Offences and Other Matters) Act 2014 (Vic)). This makes it an offence to intentionally distribute or threaten to distribute an intimate image (an image that shows sexual activity, a sexual context or the genital or anal region of a person or, in the case of a female, the breasts) and the distribution must be 'contrary to community standards of acceptable conduct'. This is defined to take into account matters such as the nature and content of the image, how it was captured and distributed, and the age and vulnerability of the person depicted (s 40). A defence applies if the person depicted is not a minor and expressly or impliedly consented or could reasonably be considered to have consented to the distribution of the image or the manner in which it was distributed. There is no defence of consent in the case of a minor because of 'their greater vulnerability and need for protection' (Crimes Amendment (Sexual Offences and Other Matters) Bill 2014, Explanatory Memorandum, p. 39).

The advantage of this offence is that it applies not only to children but also to adults and so, it reduces the apparent hypocrisy of young people facing more severe consequences for behaviour that adults engage in with apparent impunity. While the consent of a child does not excuse the distribution the requirement that the distribution or threat of distribution be done in a way that is contrary to community standards is designed to allow a flexible approach to whether a young person who sexts is charged with this offence. The danger of such a specific offence is that it could lead to net-widening because a new offence that is appropriately labelled and seemingly fits sexting scenarios may be seen as the correct response to sexting rather than diverting the child from criminal prosecution. Such concerns were raised by Neil Paterson, Acting Commander of Victoria Police (2012, p. 16), who argued that police discretion was a useful way of dealing with sexting.

LEGISLATIVE FRAMEWORK IN EUROPE

Council of Europe and European Union

In Europe, child pornography legislation has been adopted both at the supranational (Council of Europe and European Union) level and in national jurisdictions. The Council of Europe has adopted two important conventions that address child pornography in a number of provisions: the 2001 Budapest Convention on Cybercrime and the 2007 Lanzarote Convention on the Protection of Children against Sexual Exploitation and Sexual Abuse. The latter defines child pornography as 'any material that visually depicts a child engaged in real or simulated sexually explicit conduct or any depiction of a child's sexual organs for primarily sexual purposes' (article 20 (2)). This definition is very similar to the one in the Protocol under the UNCRC and, hence, could also be interpreted as being applicable to sexting between children. Yet, at the time of the adoption of the Lanzarote Convention, there was already an awareness that taking and sharing of intimate pictures was occurring between minors, and that in certain circumstances it would not be appropriate to criminalise such behaviour. This is reflected in the third paragraph of article 20 which asserts that Member States can decide that sexting between minors that have reached the age of sexual consent,[6] at least as far as this concerns the production and possession of images, should be excluded from child pornography legislation. It is added that this should only apply '*where these images are produced and possessed by them with their consent and solely for their own private use*'. However, the wording of the article also implies that sexting between minors that have not reached this age or the offering, making available, distributing, transmitting, procuring or knowingly obtaining access to this type of material, could still fall within the scope of the national child pornography laws.

A very similar approach was adopted by the European Union in its 2011 Directive on combating the sexual abuse and sexual exploitation of children and child pornography[7] in article 8 (3).[8] Recital 20 of the Directive emphasis that it 'does not govern Member States' policies with regard to consensual sexual activities in which children may be involved and which can be regarded as the normal discovery of sexuality in the course of human development, taking account of the different cultural and legal traditions and of new forms of establishing and maintaining relations among children and adolescents, including through information and communication technologies'. This can again be interpreted as a signal that Member States may exclude 'unproblematic' sexting, i.e. types of consensual sexting (limited to production, acquisition and possession) between children that have reached the age of sexual consent,[9] from child pornography legislation. According to a 2016 implementation report by the European Commission,[10] only Austria, Cyprus, Germany, Finland, Croatia and the United Kingdom have chosen to apply article 8 (3) (European Commission, 2016).[11] However, this does not automatically imply that in other Member States child pornography legislation is effectively applied to minors. Often, the particular circumstances and the child's best interests will be taken into account.

Recent Developments at National Level

Aside from the potential applicability of child pornography legislation to sexting, a trend towards the criminalisation of non-consensual dissemination of sexual images is noticeable in an increasing number of European countries. In the United Kingdom, on 13 April 2015 the amended Criminal Justice and Courts Act entered into force, which considers the disclosure of a private sexual photograph or film an offence if the disclosure is made (a) without the consent of an individual who appears in the photograph or film, and (b) with the intention of causing that individual distress (sections 33–35).[12] In Belgium, a new provision was introduced in the Criminal Code in the beginning of 2016. Article 371/1 now imposes a criminal sanction, more specifically, imprisonment of six months to five years, on the 'showing, rendering accessible or disseminating an image or sound recording of a nude person or a person involved in an explicit sexual act, without that person's consent or unbeknownst to that person, even if that person consented to the making of the recording'.[13] By focusing on the lack of consent of the person pictured, article 371/1 recognises the agency of the victim rather than the intent of the perpetrator (Beyens & Lievens, 2016). Similar provisions have been introduced in the French Penal Code (Article 226-2-1), and by the Scottish Abusive Behaviour and Sexual Harm (Scotland) Act 2016.

Although these provisions are not specifically targeted at minors or children, these provisions could be helpful in circumstances where sexting images are further shared or disseminated online without their consent.

What Legal Response Is Appropriate to Sexting by Young People?

From a legal perspective it is crucial to approach sexting in a differentiated manner that takes the specific circumstances into account. Sexting may be engaged in in a voluntary manner, with consent of all parties involved. In this context, sexting can be part of minors' legitimate exploration of their sexual identity and a way to express their sexual individuality (Livingstone & Mason, 2015). Taking and sharing intimate images can be considered part of growing up and the road to adulthood (Bond, 2014; Kimpel, 2010). This behaviour could be conceived as falling within the scope of a child's freedom of expression[14] and right to privacy,[15] which includes the right to a private sexual life (Gillespie, 2013).[16] Hence, in such circumstances sexting should not be problematised nor be dealt with by applying criminal legislation. This does not mean that awareness-raising on the exploration of sexual identity by means of technology, the importance of consent therein and potential adverse consequences should not be promoted and embedded in sexual education and media literacy initiatives.

On the other hand, sexting may be part of sexual abuse or sexual exploitation or happen under significant (peer-)pressure or coercion (Ringrose, Gill, Livingstone, & Harvey, 2012). Moreover harm may occur when images are further distributed without the consent of the person pictured. In situations where children inflict harm on other children, authorities should – as far as possible - pursue restorative approaches that repair the harm done instead of criminalising children or treating them as perpetrators. Criminalisation and prosecution should always remain the last resort. However, in certain cases the application of criminal legislation may be justified and appropriate. Yet, if all actors that are involved are minors, the use of targeted provisions, such as those recently adopted by Victoria, Australia and a number of European legislators, are to be preferred above applying child pornography legislation, as the rationale of the latter is to punish adult perpetrators that intend to sexually abuse children.

In any case, in situations where sexting images are further disseminated in a non-consensual manner, victim-blaming should be avoided. All too often victims are blamed of being 'reckless' and 'gullible', and even having enabled or provoked the dissemination of the pictures (Henry & Powell, 2015), for instance in the case of sexual(ised) selfies. Instead the focus should be shifted to the person who has disseminated the images without consent. Though this might seem self-evident, it is remarkable how often it is questioned whether the traditional limits of consent also apply in relation to the dissemination of sexual images, and sexual selfies in particular. Photos that are forwarded or posted on platforms without consent can spread quickly and cause harm both in the private and public (such as school setting) spheres of victims. Emphasising the importance of 'consent' related to any form of sexual behaviour should thus be an essential element in sexual education programmes (Livingstone & Mason, 2015). Alerting young people in such programmes to the fact that criminal provisions exist (if that is the case in their jurisdiction) for the non-consensual dissemination of sexual images could have a preventive and deterrent effect. Building resilience and teaching children not to be afraid to refuse to send someone an intimate image if this does not feel right is also essential. In this regard, innovative apps are being developed, for instance by youth helplines such as Childline,[17] to help and empower young people to formulate witty but forceful comebacks when pressured for nude images by peers.

In addition, other mechanisms and actors can and should play a role in addressing and preventing harm (Henry & Powell, 2016; Powell, 2009). Internet platforms and other channels through which images are often disseminated (such as mobile apps) should offer effective and easy-to-use reporting mechanisms, act quickly when it appears that intimate images have been posted or shared without consent, and provide transparent feedback on how reports have been addressed or dealt with. Large players have recently announced new strategies to tackle the non-consensual dissemination of sexual images. As far as Facebook is concerned, this includes checking of reports by 'specially trained representatives' and use of 'photo-matching' technology in order to prevent re-uploading of pictures and further sharing (Hern, 2017). Such strategies are not targeted at young people specifically, but at the Facebook population in general. Whereas of course these measures will also prove helpful in sexting situations between minors, companies should offer information and measures that are child-friendly, age-appropriate and easily understandable by children as well. According to the *Children's rights and business principles*, drafted by the UN Global Compact, Unicef and Save the Children in 2013 (Unicef, 2013), '*respecting and supporting children's rights requires business to both prevent harm and actively safeguard children's interests*' (Unicef, 2013, p. 3). Businesses are called upon to guarantee that products and services are safe and aim to support children's rights through them (Lievens, 2016).

Implementing children's rights in practice, not only by industry, but also by government actors, educators and parents requires attention to the full range of children's rights: their right to protection from harm, but also their right to freedom of (sexual) expression and privacy. In drafting and developing policies at all possible levels (policy, schools, families) it is essential to listen to young people themselves and let them participate in a meaningful way. This right is attributed to them in article 12 of the UNCRC. Furthermore, policies, and certainly government policies, should be informed by evidence. Hence, in-depth research into sexting practices among minors, motivations and consequences is essential, as is a transparent assessment and evaluation of practices by the various law enforcement actors in order to detect gaps in the legal framework or the need for legislative amendments.

Conclusion

This chapter has shown that sexting can cover a relatively broad range of activities, some much more problematic than others. Unsurprisingly this means that jurisdictions are grappling with how best to respond to sexting by young people and debating whether, and what sort of legal response, might be appropriate. Some jurisdictions are refusing to close the door on the possibility of prosecuting young people for child pornography offences, regardless of whether children are actually being currently prosecuted. Other more recent responses include the development of sexting specific offences which target the non-consensual distribution of intimate images. This chapter has noted that there may well be cases where a legal response is necessary but where this is the case this should take the form of a sexting specific offence focusing on the behaviour of the distributor and harm caused by the non-consensual distribution of an intimate image. Despite the existence of such formal legal responses many jurisdictions appear to divert young people from formal criminal proceedings in recognition that a formal response will rarely be necessary or appropriate. In many cases though sexting may well be a normal part of young people exploring their sexuality and while this does not preclude the existence of unforeseen problematic consequences these are best addressed through non-legal measures. Developing mechanisms to quickly and effectively respond to problematic forms of sexting is important but most vital is the deployment of young person relevant education programmes to help young people to safely negotiate the on-line world in which they increasingly live their lives.

Notes

1. Although a problematic term in many ways, because it is used to refer to a wide range of behaviours engaged in by young people and is generally not a term used by young people (see for instance Crofts, 2015; Moran-Ellis, 2012, p. 116; Weins, 2014, pp. 3–8).
2. For a discussion of what images may be thought to be, or not be, sexting and the interplay between sexuality, gender and self-representation, see Albury (2015).
3. See Crofts et al. (2015) for a study of the practices and motivations of young people concerning in sexting in Australia.
4. For research on legal responses in the United States, see Sacco, Argudin, Maguire, & Tallon (2010), McLaughlin (2012), and Sweeny (2014); in Canada, see Slane (2013).
5. There was already a limited defence available only for possession of child pornography. The recommended defences were based on existing defences in Tasmania whereby it is a defence to offences involving a child in the production of child exploitation material, producing, accessing or possessing (but not distributing) child exploitation material to prove that the material depicts sexual activity between the accused and a person under 18 that is not unlawful (Criminal Code (Tas), s130E(2)).
6. The age of sexual consent is not harmonised in the Convention, but determined by each signatory at national level.
7. The Directive defines 'child pornography' as "(i) any material that visually depicts a child engaged in real or simulated sexually explicit conduct; (ii) any depiction of the sexual organs of a child for primarily sexual purposes; (iii) any material that visually depicts any person appearing to be a child engaged in real or simulated sexually explicit conduct or any depiction of the sexual organs of any person appearing to be a child, for primarily sexual purposes; or realistic images of a child engaged in sexually explicit conduct or realistic images of the sexual organs of a child, for primarily sexual purposes". A 2015 Survey on the transposition of the Directive found that there 'are great disparities in the way Member States have implemented the term child pornography into their national laws' (Missing Children Europe, ECPAT, & eNACSO, 2015).
8. Article 8 (3): It shall be within the discretion of Member States to decide whether Article 5(2) and (6) apply to the production, acquisition or possession of material involving children who have reached the age of sexual consent where that material is produced and possessed with the consent of those children and only for the private use of the persons involved, in so far as the acts did not involve any abuse.

9. Within the EU, the age of sexual consent varies from 14 to 18 years of age (European Commission, 2016).
10. Unfortunately, implementation reports on the Lanzarote Convention do not address the transposition of article 20 (3). The Lanzarote Committee, however, has announced that the subject of their second monitoring round will explicitly address 'The dangerous effects of the child's interaction through information and communication technologies (ICT)'.
11. However, France has opted only to apply article 8(3) to the production of child pornography.
12. Section 33-35 of the Criminal Justice and Courts Act, http://www.legislation.gov.uk/ukpga/2015/2/section/33?view=extent&timeline=true
13. Translation by the authors.
14. Article 13 United Nations Convention on the Rights of the Child – UNCRC; and article 10 European Convention on Human Rights (ECHR).
15. Article 16 UNCRC and article 8 ECHR.
16. This has been acknowledged by the European Court of Human Rights (ECtHR), e.g. Dudgeon v. United Kingdom, 22 October 1981.
17. More information on the Zipit app is available at https://www.childline.org.uk/info-advice/bullying-abuse-safety/online-mobile-safety/sexting/zipit-app/

References

Albury, K. (2015). Selfies, sexts, and sneaky hats: Young people's understandings of gendered practices of self-representation. *International Journal of Communication, 9*, 1734–1745.

Beyens, J., & Lievens, E. (2016). A legal perspective on the non-consensual dissemination of sexual images: Identifying strengths and weaknesses of legislation in the US, UK and Belgium. *International Journal of Law Crime and Justice, 47*, 31–43.

Bond, E. (2011). The mobile phone = bike shed? Children, sex and mobile phones. *New Media Society, 13*, 587–604.

Bond, E. (2014). *Childhood, mobile technologies and everyday experiences: Changing childhoods.* London: Palgrave Macmillan.

Commonwealth of Australia. (2016). The senate legal and constitutional affairs references committee, phenomenon colloquially referred to as 'revenge porn'. Retrieved from http://www.aph.gov.au/Parliamentary_Business/Committees/Senate/Legal_and_Constitutional_Affairs/Revenge_porn/Report

Crofts, T., & Lee, M. (2013). 'Sexting', children and child pornography. *Sydney Law Review, 35*(1), 85–106.

Crofts, T., Lee, M., McGovern, A., & Milivojevic, S. (2015). *Sexting and young people*. Basingstoke, UK: Palgrave Macmillan.

Cumming, P. (2009). *Children's rights, children's voices, children's technology, children's sexuality*. Paper presented at Roundtable on youth, sexuality, technology, Carleton University, 26 May 2009. Retrieved from http://www.yorku.ca/cummingp/documents/TeenSextingbyPeterCummingMay262009.pdf

De Ridder, S. (2017). Mediatization and sexuality: An invitation to a deep conversation on values, communicative sexualities, politics and media. Retrieved from http://www.lse.ac.uk/media@lse/research/mediaWorkingPapers/pdf/WP42-FINAL.pdf

European Commission. (2016). Report from the Commission to the European Parliament and the Council assessing the extent to which the Member States have taken the necessary measures in order to comply with Directive 2011/93/EU of 13 December 2011 on combating the sexual abuse and sexual exploitation of children and child pornography, COM(2016)871 final. Retrieved from http://eur-lex.europa.eu/legal-content/EN/TXT/PDF/?uri=CELEX:52016DC0871&qid=1491986506397&from=EN

Gillespie, A. (2010). Legal definitions of child pornography. *Journal of Sexual Aggression, 16*, 19–31.

Gillespie, A. (2013). Adolescents, sexting and human rights. *Human Rights Law Review, (4)*, 623–643.

Henry, N., & Powell, A. (2015). Beyond the 'sext': Technology-facilitated sexual violence and harassment against adult women. *Australia & New Zealand Journal of Criminology, 48*, 104–118.

Henry, N., & Powell, A. (2016). Sexual violence in the digital age – The scope and limits of criminal law. *Social Legal Studies, 12*, 1–22. Retrieved from http://sls.sagepub.com/content/early/2016/01/11/0964663915624273.abstract

Hern, A. (2017, April 5). Facebook launching tools to tackle revenge porn. *The Guardian*. Retrieved from https://www.theguardian.com/technology/2017/apr/05/facebook-tools-revenge-porn

Kimpel, A. (2010). Using laws designed to protect as a weapon: Prosecuting minors under child pornography laws. *New York University Review of Law & Social Change, 34*, 299–338.

Law Reform Committee of Victoria (VLRC). (2013). *Parliament of Victoria, inquiry into sexting*. Report of the Law Reform Committee for the inquiry into sexting, Parliamentary paper No. 230, Session 2010–2013.

Lee, M., & Crofts, T. (2015). Gender, pressure, coercion and pleasure: Untangling motivations for sexting between young people. *The British Journal of Criminology, 55*(3), 454–473.

Lievens, E. (2014). Bullying and sexting in social networks: Protecting minors from criminal acts or empowering minors to cope with risky behaviour? *International Journal of Crime, Law & Justice, 42*(3), 251–270.

Lievens, E. (2016). Is self-regulation failing children and young people? Assessing the use of alternative regulatory instruments in the area of social networks. In S. Simpson, H. Van den Bulck, & M. Puppis (Eds.), *European media policy for the twenty-first century: Assessing the past, setting agendas for the future* (pp. 77–94). New York: Routledge.

Livingstone, S., & Mason, J. (2015). *Sexual rights and sexual risks among youth online*. A review of existing knowledge regarding children and young people's developing sexuality in relation to new media environments. http://www.enacso.eu/wp-content/uploads/2015/10/eNACSO-Review-on-Sexual-rights-and-sexual-risks-among-online-youth.pdf

Makkai, T. in Krone, T. (2005). *Does thinking make it so? Defining online child pornography possession offences*. Trends & Issues in Crime and Criminal Justice No 299, Australian Institute of Criminology.

McGrath, H. (2009). *Young people and technology: A review of the current literature* (2nd ed.). South Melbourne, VIC: Alannah and Madeline Foundation. Retrieved from http://www.ncab.org.au/Assets/Files/2ndEdition_Youngpeopleandtechnology_LitReview_June202009.pdf.

McLaughlin, J. (2012). Exploring the first amendment rights of teens in relationship to sexting and censorship. *University of Michigan Journal of Law Reform, 45*(2), 315–350.

Missing Children Europe, ECPAT and eNACSO. (2015). A survey on the transposition of Directive 2011/93/EU on combating sexual abuse and sexual exploitation of children and child pornography. Retrieved from http://missing-childreneurope.eu/Portals/0/Docs/A%20survey%20on%20transposition%20of%20Directive%20against%20child%20sexual%20exploitation%20and%20abuse.pdf

Moran-Ellis, J. (2012). Sexting, intimacy and criminal acts: Translating teenage sexualities. In P. Johnson & D. Dalton (Eds.), *Policing sex* (pp. 115–131). London: Routledge.

O'Connor, B. (2010). *Debate on crimes legislation amendment (Sexual offences against children) Bill 2010*. Commonwealth, *Parliamentary Debates*, House of Representatives, 9 March 2010, p. 2052.

Ostrager, B. (2010). SMS. OMG! LOL! TTYL: Translating the law to accommodate today's teens and the evolution from texting to sexting. *Family Court Review, 48*(4), 712–726.

Powell, A. (2009). New technologies, unauthorised visual images and sexual assault. *ACSSA Aware, 23*, 6–12. Retrieved from http://www.academia.edu/1985860/New_technologies_unauthorised_visual_images_and_sexual_assault.

Ringrose, J., Gill, R., Livingstone, S., & Harvey, L. (2012). A qualitative study of children, young people and 'sexting' – A report prepared for the NSPCC,

2012. Retrieved from http://www.nspcc.org.uk/Inform/resourcesforprofessionals/sexualabuse/sexting-research-report_wdf89269.pdf

Rosenberg, E. (2011) In Weiner's wake, a brief history of the word "sexting". *The Wire*, Retrieved from http://www.thewire.com/national/2011/06/brief-history-sexting/38668/

Sacco, D. T., Argudin, R., Maguire, J., & Tallon, K. (2010). Sexting: Youth practices and legal implications, Cyberlaw clinic, Harvard Law School. Retrieved from http://cyber.law.harvard.edu/sites/cyber.law.harvard.edu/files/Sacco_Argudin_Maguire_Tallon_Sexting_Jun2010.pdf

Slane, A. (2013). Sexting and the law in Canada. *Canadian Journal of Human Sexuality, 22*(3), 117–122.

Sweeny, J. (2014). Sexting and freedom of expression: A comparative approach. *Kentucky Law Journal, 102*(1), 103–146.

Taylor, M., Holland, G., & Quayle, E. (2001). Typology of paedophile picture collections. *Police Journal, 74*, 97–107.

Taylor, M., & Quayle, E. (2003). *Child pornography: An internet crime.* Hove, UK: Brunner-Routledge.

Unicef. (2013). Children's rights and business principles. Retrieved from http://www.unglobalcompact.org/docs/issues_doc/human_rights/CRBP/Childrens_Rights_and_Business_Principles.pdf

Weins, W. J. (2014). In T. C. Hiestand & W. J. Weins (Eds.), *Sexting and youth: A multidisciplinary examination of research, theory, and law* (pp. 3–8). Durham, NC: Carolina Academic Press.

Index[1]

---

[1] Note: Page numbers followed by 'n' refer to notes.

© The Author(s) 2018   137
M. Walrave et al. (eds.), *Sexting*, Palgrave Studies in Cyberpsychology,
https://doi.org/10.1007/978-3-319-71882-8